Faith and Love

Faith and Love

SHAMANE

authorHOUSE®

AuthorHouse™
1663 Liberty Drive
Bloomington, IN 47403
www.authorhouse.com
Phone: 1-800-839-8640

First published by AuthorHouse   01/04/2012

ISBN: 978-1-4685-4074-1 (sc)
ISBN: 978-1-4685-4073-4 (hc)
ISBN: 978-1-4685-4072-7 (ebk)

Library of Congress Control Number: 2012900138

Printed in the United States of America

Any people depicted in stock imagery provided by Thinkstock are models, and such images are being used for illustrative purposes only.
Certain stock imagery © Thinkstock.

This book is printed on acid-free paper.

INTRODUCTION

A person's life allows him to exist because of the purpose he tries to attain, Pushed by the faith in whatever he believes, and the love or lack of, that he acquires along the way to sustain his time.

'Faith and Love' is a compilation of two short stories about life. "The Girl in the Peach Dress", is a young girl's journey through losing parents and hard work to finding kinfolk and love. "Naj", is love in a Muslim home. It is one woman's journey through the trials of rejection and misunderstanding to finding true love in Allah and then finding her family again.

Allah, the One True God is the unifying theme of the universe. In whatever form or color we are presented, we all experience similar trials and we only differ in the way we handle them.

These stories are written to increase us in our Faith in God and good and to always have hope of happy endings.

Shamane.
December 2011

Acknowledgement

Faith is that resolute strength of belief in something,
Fate is that plan I must endure,
Love is that feeling that makes living, a smile . . .

A woman's life is entwined with the love of many
Family, friends and children . . . .

For my children I send my prayers, I give my love.
Dearest Kamilah, my son Omar, my little Zainab,
May Allah keep you safe and guided to Him always.

For my Mother, I am glad you are my mother. I love you.

For my siblings, we are one crazy bunch, but we have the love and
Allah and I pray it stays that way.

For my friends, wherever you are, keep the faith, share the love.

If I have offended anyone, please forgive me, it was/is not my intention.

May our Faith in all that is good be strengthened,
May our Faith in An Almighty God be renewed and sustained,
May our love be true in whatever way we give it and however we receive,
May Our Creator be pleased with us all. Ameen

For all those who have known love in any little way.

It is a Blessed and Beautiful sharing.

And especially for you my Sweet Baby,

You have my love.

GIRL IN A
PEACH DRESS

CHAPTER ONE

The Big Shop

It was cool and light at half past five on a Sunday morning. Even the rooster slept in and forgot to crow but Kaddy was up and happy. She was eleven going on twelve but looking like a wiry eight with long legs and thin cheeks. Not much of a child to be noticed until you saw her eyes. Beautiful medium brown pupils that showed happiness and mischief, sadness and anger, but a definite kindness that made others smile. Kaddy never knew her father. All that she was and learned as a child came from her mother. Her "Mamam" was beautiful and kind and warm. She taught her good manners and how to pray and how to be quiet, yet strong. Kaddy's mummy died when Kaddy was only nine years old. Kaddy was taken by her mother's brother Uncle to live with him, his wife Molly and their daughter Elizabeth. Uncle and Aunt Molly had a big shop which would have been a treat for any child. There were jars of toffees and chewing gum balls and peppermint sticks and twizzlers and peanut brittle and milky fudge squares and coconut cakes and balloons and buttons . . . . The freezers were full of all colors of ice cream and juices and icicle pops. And there were cakes . . . Kaddy loved the smell of the cup cakes and the jam rolls and the pinetarts and the brownies.

And there was fresh bread . . . long soft plaited loaves and short fat sliced loaves. And there was so much more . . . Barrels of flour, and sugar and salt and rice and peas and were lined together each with a shiny aluminum scoop. Overhead packed on shelves up to the roof, were cans and cans of everything that came in a can. Huge trays of onions and garlic and potatoes and smoked herrings and salted snappers, lay covered protected from greedy flies. And there was still more. In beautiful glass covered cupboards there were clothes for little girls and mummies, and pretty soft cloth and thread and needles and laces and braids and creams and perfumes and lotions and powder and still more lay around a corner, toys and books and chalk and pencils and games and more . . . Uncle and Aunt Molly were established as the village store owners. Every day except on Sunday they opened for business from seven in the morning to eight at night. Aunt Molly served the customers. Uncle would buy all the stuff and he and Old Man Pa would fetch and pack them into the shop. There was Aunty Pam who cooked and cleaned upstairs where the family lived. There was Uncle and Aunt Molly's twelve year old daughter Elizabeth who did nothing but take candy from the big glass jars and then there was Kaddy who had to clean up the Big Shop on Sundays. She was up early. She had brushed her teeth and fixed her hair and said her prayers for a new day as Mamam had taught her. She closed her door quietly without locking it and made her way down the back stairs to the Big Iron Doors of the Big Shop. Old man Pa was the old gardener/ guard/handyman. He lived in a small shed at the back of the yard. He was already up and had opened the locks on the Big iron Grills that protected the Big Iron Doors. "Hi there little Missy!" he called out to Kaddy. "You up early!" Kaddy smiled. She got her cloth, bucket and broom and entered a world of Shop smells. She liked cleaning. Mother had taught her to put things in order and in their place. She made sure all the candies were sorted, all the jars dusted and shiny and all lined up neatly. Barrels of sugar and rice and flour were scraped and dusted and covered tightly. Counters were cleaned. Everything that was shifted had to be put back in its place. It was then simple dusting and sweeping and piling up the trash. Kaddy had it all organized. There was one part of the Shop that Kaddy did not like. She wished she did not have to smell the trays of onions, garlic, potatoes and fish. There was always something rotting or going bad. She would see Aunt Molly pushing out the bad skins on the rotting onions and saving the hard cores. Then she would chop off the bad potato parts and put the good halves and quarters in a new tray to be sold first the next day. There was nothing as horrible smelling Kaddy concluded as a rotten potato until you came across a dead big rat. A shop like that attracted big rats. Uncle and Old Man Pa had trained a dog called Harper to smell out and chase and kill the big rats. But sometimes Harper would bite them and they would run away under the wooden stacks that held the sacks of goods and there die. It was horrible ugly smelly for 4 days. If Old Man Pa could reach it he would take the rotting things out but most times it had to be endured. Old Man Pa would laugh in his toothless shaking head chuckle and say, "Sniff some perfume Missy and in four days it all rotted and dried." Kaddy worked as quickly and properly as she could. She remembered songs her mother used to sing. Kaddy sang as she worked, free and loud and alone in the Big Shop. She was glad it was Sunday. She was glad Aunt Molly and Elizabeth were asleep. Aunt Pam was probably upstairs preparing breakfast. Kaddy looked at the big clock in the Big Shop. It was already 830am. Everything was clean and in order. Two hours had gone by very quickly. She just had to get the last bit of dust into the Big Bin. Old Man Pa would help take the bin out to the back. She was a little scared of Old Man Pa. He was wrinkled and thin and had no teeth and he looked Old . . . . like two hundred years old! But he looked out for her and he called her "little Missy". Kaddy liked that. He called Elizabeth, Queen Elizabeth but he always laughed when he said it so Kaddy felt that her "little Missy" title was more royal and respectful. As the last bit of dust was dumped, Kaddy went into the yard to find the old handyman. He heard her calling and soon came to get the Big Bin. He took her bucket and broom from her and told her to get cleaned up. Kaddy cleaned up at the pipe in the yard then after shaking off the water she took her time up the back stairs to the Big House upstairs.

Aunt Pam was in the kitchen. 'Morning Aunt Pam!" Kaddy called out quietly to the busy Aunt Pam. "Hi yourself Squeak!" Aunt Pam said. "You finished downstairs?" "Yes Aunt Pam", Kaddy replied as she looked at the pile of pancakes in the kitchen. "Do you want your breakfast now?" Aunt Pam asked. "You can eat it in your room." "Yes please," Kaddy told her and she waited quietly as Aunt Pam got busy. She was not too sure of or close to Aunt Pam. They respected each other as people in the Big House but Aunt Pam's loyalties were clearly for miss Queen Elizabeth and her Highness Miss Molly. Sometimes she would detect extra kindness and understanding from Aunt Pam but Kaddy kept to herself and her room when she was upstairs in the Big House. Sunday mornings were for Uncle, Aunt Molly and their precious daughter. They sat together and had breakfast together. Kaddy accepted her place in the household. She was glad when they had their time together. She collected her plate of fried ripe plantains, pancakes with syrup and soft scrambled eggs and a small glass of orange juice from Aunt Pam and took herself to her room next to the kitchen. Kaddy could hear snores at 9.00am on a Sunday. Maybe there would be peace for another hour. Kaddy wanted to enjoy every minute of it. Kaddy was hungry. Two hours of cleaning was hard work. She ate quickly and tongue cleaned her plate. She knew it was bad manners but she had to get all of the thick syrup. Aunt Pam had given her two pancakes. Kaddy could eat two more but why wish. Her mother used to tell her not to be greedy. "Be contented my baby", she would say "Life is not easy but things will work out alright". Mamam used to make pancakes, soft and fluffy and she made her own syrup with spices. Kaddy could eat as many as her tummy wanted. Then her mother used to clean her up and hug her tightly and they would make plans for the day. Kaddy sat in the middle of her little bed and folded her legs under her. She remembered her mother's laugh and her smile and the way she smelled like fresh flowers. Kaddy missed her mother. Suddenly the pancakes and plantains felt as if they were up at her throat. She missed Mamam. Kaddy wrapped her own thin arms around herself and looked at the pattern on the sheet. She did not want her Own anything, not clothes or books or jewelry, how she wished her own mother was alive. Kaddy started to cry. Mamam had died and was gone so quickly and she was moved into this life. She wished Elizabeth was not so mean, she wished she could hug Uncle, he was her mother's brother. She wished she could be close to Aunt Molly but Aunt Molly did not want to be close to her. She was all alone at eleven. She did not know of any other uncles or aunts or grandparents. Many times she wondered why it all happened to her but her mother's voice was strict with that reasoning. "Never you ask why Sweetie. Don't question God's plan. Ask Him for help to get through each day and He will help." Kaddy cleaned up her face and took the dishes out to Aunt Pam. "Thank You Aunt Pam", she said to the busy cook. Aunt Pam gave a sound of acknowledgement and turned to take the dishes. "What happened to you?" Aunt Pam said as she saw the weepy eyes and wet nose. It was not a question to be answered. Kaddy went back to room.

CHAPTER TWO

A Suitor for Lizze

It was just the beginning of the day. Kaddy had much work from school to get done. She often thought about her schooling and she was happy she was allowed to go to school. Aunt Molly insisted the first day Kaddy got to the Big House. She said she had no time to baby sit a strange child all day. It was arranged that Kaddy join the same school Elizabeth was attending. They both used the same school bus but Elizabeth let it be known that Kaddy was the poor relative, without a mother or a father, who lived off her parents. Kaddy did not care. She was trying to learn all she could in her classes. She liked books and she liked to study. She wished she had more time with her books. She helped Aunt Molly every day after school in the shop. Sometimes her legs were so tired she would go to sleep without taking any dinner. She had placed Second and Third in her Class in the last two years but she was not taken to any of her year end graduations. There was no mention at any time about "Queen Elizabeth's" grades.

That Sunday moved into Monday and many Sundays after that. The clock ticked and life moved along to catch up. Three years had just happened. Kaddy was now in the final year at her school. Elizabeth had completed her schooling and she had taken other classes in computer studies. Uncle bought her a new computer system and she sat in front of the monitor for most of the day chatting with friends and listening to music with ear phones in her ears. Kaddy was helping more with the customers in the Big Shop. She was glad she could help Aunt Molly. She was able to take a nap in the afternoon as Kaddy opened the shop and took over the ordering and stocking and the accounts. Old Man Pa had died in his sleep and so it was Uncle who spent more time in the Shop now. Kaddy passed her finals with three distinctions and three credits. (3A'sand 3B's) She got a little hug from Aunt Molly but no gifts. She was happy with the hug. Uncle told her Mamam would be proud. Life had settled into a relaxed pace. Aunt Pam had left for another country so under Aunt Molly's tutoring Kaddy became a very good cook. She cooked for the family all the time. She also did the house cleaning as well as the Shop cleaning. They had all grown up. Uncle's hair was turning silver. Aunt Molly's hips were aching. Kaddy was 18 and Elizabeth was 20. Uncle announced one day after dinner, "Moll, its time to get Lizze married." Elizabeth jumped up from the computer desk and held her father around the middle. "Daddy!" she cried out in a half gleeful shy manner. She actually agreed. Elizabeth wanted to get married. Aunt Molly suddenly blossomed minus ten years in youth. She had a new project. She had a mission to get a good suitor for Elizabeth. For the next year there was unity of purpose in the Big Shop Household. Suitors were sent by 'wise' Old Aunts and Concerned Grandmas. Elizabeth was groomed and dressed and adorned and proudly displayed. Sometimes the Meetings were so comical Uncle could not wait for the shy or over anxious applicants to leave, so he could start laughing. He shook his head as soon as he saw most of them. "Boys! Boys!", he would tell Aunt Molly. "They are not ready for our Lizze."

One Sunday after the visitor left Kaddy cleaned up early and went to her room. She sat on her tiny warm faithful bed and looked into the mirror on the little vanity. She was a young lady, slender to thin, five feet six inches tall, one hundred and twenty five pounds in weight, with long black bouncy hair and dancing brown eyes. She had her mother's solid smooth fair skin. Kaddy leaned forward to look more closely at the face in the mirror. There were neat thick eyebrows over long dark eyelashes, a straight pretty nose and a not too long pretty face. "I am pretty", Kaddy thought. She was educated, well versed in the mechanics of Shop upkeep and trade and keeping accounts. She could cook and bake and manage a household. She had good manners and she prayed and fasted often.

Kaddy made up her Resume of Eligibility in her mind and smiled to the mirror. What was to become of her? After Lizze was married and gone would Kaddy have to continue in the Big Shop? Would she ever leave the Big House? Would Uncle or Aunt Molly ever say, "Its time to get Kaddy married."

Ah Well! Snap out of it! Kaddy told herself. What do you know of boys and men anyway? In her busy life Kaddy never had the time to stop to think. The boys at school kept their distance and the boys in the Village never tried any advances. Everyone everywhere seemed to know that she was Kaddy the orphan girl that had to be taken in. Who would want her? But Kaddy knew that one day she would like to be in love. She prayed for a young man who would look at her and love her and only her. Mamam used to sing pieces of love songs. Kaddy could remember her mother telling her about how handsome her father was. Mamam would be happy when she spoke and then she would get very sad. She never explained what happened to daddy. Kaddy had found a card among her mother's things. It was a cardboard heart Someone had made with crayons and in the heart were written the words, "Andrew loves Haley". Kaddy's mother was Haley and her father was Andrew. Kaddy knew that Haley really loved that Andrew until she died.

CHAPTER THREE

Meet Andy Pero

And so it was, that what is written, must take its due turn. It began like a normal Friday. Uncle got a phone call from relatives about another prospective suitor for Lizze. The young man was trained in the Big Industrial World and he had returned to his village to find a suitable bride. He and his family wanted to see Lizze later that evening. Aunt Molly rushed Kaddy upstairs away from Shop duty to prepare snacks and dinner for the guests. Uncle closed the Big Shop early and they all got busy. Elizabeth fussed with her hair and could not decide what to wear. After some time she appeared from her trampled bedroom in a long black skirt and a sky blue Indian cotton top. She wore long tear drop golden earrings, matching necklace and jingly golden bangles on her wrists. Her recently permed shoulder length light brown hair was kept away from her face with a pale blue bandeau. Light lipgloss accentuated her full lips and generous sprays of Avon Rare Pearls completed the ensemble. Her toenails and fingers were touched up with natural nail polish. She looked fresh and ready. Uncle put on a good white long sleeved shirt over a comfortable pair of khaki pants. Aunt Molly slipped into one of her 'Designer' dresses. They all got busy arranging the living room with the good cushions and fancy side lights and . . . Kaddy glanced a couple times from her station in the kitchen to the bustling preparations. Kaddy smiled. She had managed to get fried chicken strips and heaps of fried green and ripe plantains unto a large platter with dips of mayonnaise and mustard and ketchup and pickles. There was macaroni and cheese in the oven and warming garlic bread. That and some grilled steaks and a kissable crunchy garden salad was the dinner idea. She had brought up a chocolaty chocolate cake and a lemon pie cake to go with ice cream for dessert. There was cool lime and lemon drink over ice cubes to go with the chicken strip platter to be served when they arrived. The coffee pot was fresh. The tea kettle was whistling. All the trays were prepared. All the plates were cleaned and all the napkins folded. Things were ready in the kitchen.

Kaddy washed her hands and looked down at what she had on. It was a light peach dress Aunt Molly had given to her from the Shop because it was "too plain" and would "not sell". Little puffed sleeves and peach ribbon at the neckline were the only embellishments to a midcalf length of peachy peach silk. It did look plain but it was simple and statuly too. It was graceful and since it was not a Lizze hand—me-down, Kaddy felt special in it. She had been working all afternoon wearing it but Kaddy just smoothed it out with her hands and shrugged her shoulders. No bother! She was not the one to be shown off. She waited in the kitchen. That was the rule whenever suitors came. Kaddy was to stay in the kitchen or her room. Soon enough the visitors arrived. They came in two fancy shiny cars. The young man drove himself and from his car alighted his parents and grandmother. From the other car out came an aunt and uncle and two male cousins. The boy's mother gave Aunt Molly a nicely wrapped gift. There were hugs and handshakes and introductions. There was laughter and ease and conversation. Kaddy had been peeping past the thick drapes that separated the kitchen view from the rest of the huge long living room. As she waited she decided to make a fruit salad from some grapes, pears and a watermelon that stared at her from the kitchen counter. She cut the watermelon lengthwise into two halves and used the scooped out fruit skins as the bowls for the salad. She took her time cutting up the pears into bite sized chunks and then she added green sections of kiwi for color. She drizzled some honey over the top of it all and put the two fruit bowls into a tray of the big freezer. It was always good to have something extra to serve. Aunt Molly came past the curtains into the kitchen. She collected the platters and plates and tray of beverage and glasses. Uncle helped as the guests sampled and ate and enjoyed. The Big television was on. Cricket matches were being played somewhere in the World. They were all involved and happy. Lizzie had moved from the 'Shy just Introduced' stage to the 'Let go and be Me' stage. She liked the young suitor and they all seemed to like her. She and the young man and one of his cousins were seated on the carpet playing Monopoly. The Grandma was seated in Uncle's recliner with her feet up. Everything was served and eaten. The tender steaks and cheesy macaroni were a hit. Then ice cream and cake was served and dishes returned. For each new item the guests protested they just couldn't eat any more but they still cleaned it all up. Kaddy prepared the coffee and took the Fruit Cocktail out of the freezer.

And then it seemed, the Angels wanted to have some fun. Aunt Molly had taken the coffee in and then the house phone rang. She put the coffee pot down and went to answer the call, some distance away from the happy party. It was a call from overseas from Aunt Molly's mother. She wanted an update and Aunt Molly was bubbling in conversation. The boy's Grandma asked if she could have some fruit and Aunt Molly smiled in assurance of an accomplished Hostess. "Sure Grandma", she answered the Grandma and Aunt Molly looked over to Elizabeth and said nicely, "Lizze can you get the Fruit salad please." Elizabeth said a half hearted involved in Monopoly, "Okay Mom", and Aunt Molly turned away from the group to divulge some tasty information to her mother as she continued her talking on the phone. Elizabeth was comfortable in her acceptance and in smooth routine manner. She called to the kitchen, "Kaddy please serve the salad now." Aunt Molly tried to end the conversation on the phone but other forces were in control that hour. Kaddy was startled to hear her name being called. Then Lizzie called again and Kaddy's shy voice was heard saying, "I am coming Lizze." Kaddy balanced the half watermelon skin with its three pounds of sweet contents and pushed past the curtains to the happy people in the living room. Too many strange eyes were looking at her. There were the two male cousins and the Uncle and there was Him. He was watching as she walked and he stood up to help her. As he took the watermelon bowl his fingers gently covered hers. She pulled away and let go of the fruit. He tried to hold on to the bowl, held it to himself and fell backwards on top of Uncle and his mother on the sofa. The cousins were laughing. Uncle was drenched in syrupy pears and grapes and the mother had watermelon bits in her new hairdo. Lizzie was laughing as usual. He was laughing too and poor Aunt Molly was apologizing and trying to clean up. Kaddy took advantage of the chaos and retreated to the kitchen. Her legs were like paper stilts. Her face and chest were blushing and sweating. His touch had done that to her. His eyes had done that to her. Her head felt like there was hot steam inside And her palms were balmy. Aunt Molly came into the kitchen. "I am so sorry Aunt. I am so sorry!" was all Kaddy could say. Molly waved her hand in a gesture of, "really cant listen to anything now", and made trips with paper towels and a trash bag and spray cleaners to and from the living room. Lizze gladly took her sticky suitor and his fruit covered mother into Molly's private bathroom where they could shower and get cleaned up. She helped her mother find appropriate clothes so the guests could change. Aunt Molly tried to get the stains out and got busy laundering the soiled garments. Uncle came into the kitchen. Kaddy was wringing her hands and looked at him as pitiful as she felt. "I am so sorry Uncle. I really am." "Don't worry child," Uncle said, "Just another way to serve salad", and he chuckled his way out and back to the living room. When they were all changed and dried Kaddy heard the Grandma ask, "Who is the girl?" There were seconds of silence and then muted explanations. Kaddy sighed. She was exhausted. She slipped quietly past the kitchen to her room and locked her Door. She did not hear the happy people leave and no one bothered her that night. She fell asleep crying and dreaming of Maman and Maman's smile. Kaddy was not chastised for the incident. Aunt Molly was happily preoccupied. She liked this boy Andy Pero. He had his own car, he was an Engineer educated in the Big Country. He was also a citizen of that country and his family members owned their own businesses, homes and cars. They hit the Jackpot. They approved of this suitor. Elizabeth was caught up in the possibilities. For the next week, Aunt Molly and Uncle and Lizze were on their personal errands. They were getting Lizze ready for a wedding and a possible trip abroad. They left Kaddy to herself and she was happy. She was praying for Guidance and begging God to show her the meaning of all the happenings. Something Special happened to her when 'he' touched her. The weekend came. Kaddy was busy in the Big Shop. She closed up at 8.30pm that Saturday night and made her way up the stairs. Uncle was on the phone to the Pero family. Aunt Molly was at his elbow and Lizze sat across from them listening to every word and gesture. Uncle was saying how much he appreciated Andy and his family and he was thanking them for the gifts. Then Kaddy heard him ask when they could meet again and organize the future. The person on the other end of the call then said something to which Uncle said, "Okay, ... Okay, ... I see! . . . . Okay then! And Uncle hung up the phone. Aunt Molly and Uncle went to the sofa. "What happened Dad?" Lizze asked urgently. Uncle cast a glance over his shoulder to the direction of the kitchen where Kaddy was and then he lowered the tone of his voice and spoke to his daughter. "They think you are great and we are good parents but the boy said he is in love with someone else," Uncle told Lizze. "What!" Lizze exclaimed, "He doesn't want me!", and she ran off crying to her room. Aunt Molly was quiet. "How could they do that?", she said. "They told us he wasn't seeing anyone. How could they fool us like that?" Aunt Molly was angry and disappointed and angry some more. For the next half of an hour they watched the television both busy in thought. Meanwhile, Lizze could be heard pounding her pillow and hitting the walls in her crying tantrum. The phone rang again. Aunt Molly got up to answer it. It was Andy Pero's mother. She was upset with her son Andy. She loved Lizze. She loved Aunt Molly and Uncle. She promised she would speak with her son again and hoped that they could all meet that Sunday. Uncle grunted when Aunt Molly told him. Then she went to tell Lizze. With hope still alive, everyone slept early.

CHAPTER FOUR

Leaving the Big House

Sunday was the next day and it dawned with foreboding. The sun didn't seem to want to be awakened. Aunt Molly herself tended to the meals that day. There was roasted duck with buttered greens and brown garden rice salad and creamed sweet potato and tangy pineapple sauce. Kaddy did her chores upstairs and then went down to her cleaning in the Big Shop. She did not want to be upstairs when the visitors were there. She saw the cars arrive. She was still sweeping when she saw the cars leave. They had not stayed for lunch. That was not good. Kaddy hurried up to finish her work. She was nervous. Something was wrong. She locked up the Big Grills and made her way up the stairs. A delayed chastisement is worse than an immediate rebuke. Kaddy made her way slowly upstairs. She heard yelling and quarreling. She had never heard Aunt Molly use such loud words. As she got within sight of her Aunt, Aunt Molly pointed her hand towards Kaddy. "You! You ungrateful girl! Get her out of her!" she shouted to Uncle. Uncle tried to reason quietly with his angry wife but Aunt Molly kept saying, "I don't want her here. Take her away." A bewildered Kaddy ran to her room and collapsed unto her bed. "What had happened?" Did Aunt Molly really want her to leave? Uncle tapped lightly on the partly open door and pushed his way into Kaddy's room. "You cant stay here anymore Kaddy", he said so quietly without looking at her face. "Pack your things. I will take you to another place." He then left the pale thin child crying with her head bowed in her hands. There wasn't much to pack. Kaddy's fingers did not know how to begin packing. She pulled a small carry on suitcase from under the bed. She had rescued it from one of Miss Elizabeth's room cleaning. Most of what she had to put into it was given to her in that home. In ten minutes she was packed. Maman's precious Holy Book was put in last and Kaddy zipped it all up. Habit made her straighten the bed sheets and dust the vanity. After seven years she was leaving the little room. She had grown up in that room. She had grown up before that vanity mirror. Uncle tapped on the door again. He took the suitcase from her and told her to meet him at the car in the yard. Kaddy moved because she had to. Aunt Molly stood at the door. Kaddy looked up at the only aunt and mother she had known and in many ways loved for the last seven years. "Please forgive me Aunt, for whatever wrong I have done," Kaddy cried. "Please Aunt, Please Forgive me. Kaddy stood close beseeching her aunt. Kaddy did not know how to walk out of the door. Aunt Molly made it easy. "Go away from here!" she shouted and moved in anger towards Kaddy. Kaddy opened the door and stepped unto the stairs outside. Aunt firmly closed the door behind her. Her feet moved slowly one step at a time until she got to Uncle's car. She was leaving the Big House and the Big Shop. What lay ahead for the orphan girl?

CHAPTER FIVE

Meet Grannyma

They drove in silence for hours. Kaddy loved car rides. She loved the passing trees and vehicles and traffic lights . . . but not this time. All her crying made her sleepy. She sat back into her seat and let her fate take its course. Uncle checked her a couple times through the rear view mirror but he did not say or explain anything to her. He looked tired too. Three hours had passed and then Uncle pulled the car off the main road and unto a red dusty road. There were more trees now. Big cows walked along the side of the narrow road. Men on bicycles were passing Uncle. He waved to two of them. There were huge laden fruit trees squatting on the terrain looking at the nervous girl and her Uncle as they drove by. And suddenly they stopped. Uncle looked back and put the car into reverse gear. He had passed the place. He parked next to a wooden bridge of an unfenced yard. No one came out or looked out from the unpainted wooden building. Some chickens and ducks and an empty hammock waited to see the visitors. Uncle got Kaddy's suitcase out of the trunk of the car and moved to open the door so she could get out. He put the windows up and secured the car. He started walking towards the old wooden bridge and opened the old wooden gate. He looked towards Kaddy and she followed. He motioned with his hands for her to remain under the house while he walked towards the old wooden structures at the back of the yard. "Grannyma! Grannyma!" she heard him call. Out ran a yelping dog chased by a tall lady with a coconut broom. "Get out of here, Get out, you wicked creature," the lady screamed as she ran the dog past Uncle and over the wooden bridge. The scream turned to concern when she saw Uncle and Kaddy. "What happened Raymond?" Kaddy heard her ask Uncle. He held Grannyma's hand and moved her aside to explain.

Kaddy had not moved. She had dodged the terrified dog and stepped into a corner. All she could hear in her head were the words, "Get out. Get out!" Grannyma approached her and looked closely at her face. Kaddy stretched her arms out and hugged her. She smelled like wood and grass. "Come with me upstairs", she told Kaddy. Grannyma led the way and Kaddy walked behind her. Uncle shook the hammock free of dust and made himself comfortable. Kaddy was on her own with the dog chasing lady. There were two bedrooms, a living room with another hammock and a kitchen. There was no bathroom upstairs. "If you need to go 'little', use the potty," Grannyma explained as she pointed to a flinted half gallon sized enamel potty. "If you need to go 'serious', you have to let me take you outside. Kaddy shook her head in understanding and made a mental note. She hoped she did not have to do one or two during the night.

The house was lit by lanterns. There was one hanging in the kitchen, one in the living room and one in each bedroom. Grannyma sat on an old faded sofa and patted the seat next to her. "Come here child," She said to Kaddy. Kaddy sat as indicated. "Your Uncle Raymond has brought you to live with me. I have no problem with that. I need the company but you have to behave. You will help with the work around here. You must be regular with your prayers and fasting. Do you understand?" Kaddy listened to the quiet voice of Grannyma and shook her head in agreement with the Terms of Occupancy and Care. Grannyma continued. "Tonight, your Uncle will use that room", and she pointed to the smaller bedroom, "and you will sleep with me. When Raymond leaves you can put your things in there." Grannyma then took a lantern and made her way down old wooden steps to the downstairs. She showed Kaddy two wooden huts for bathing and toilet use. The Washing room was three feet off the main dwelling area. It was a clean six feet by six feet hut with a tiled floor. There was no shower but a bucket stood under a water pipe. A small shelf above held bottles of shampoo and a container for soap. There were nails stuck into the wooden walls for hanging clothes and towels. There was also a clean mirror. The wooden door was held in place both inside and outside by two inch hooks. At the side of this was the very important out house toilet. This was a taller wooden structure four feet by four feet and eight feet high over three feet off the ground. Someone had fitted a ceramic toilet bowl into a platform of wood. Under the platform was a huge pit dug into the earth. There was also a water pipe and a bucket to facilitate flushing and cleaning. Kaddy did not take much note then. She prayed she would not need to 'go' during the night. Uncle had taken her suitcase inside and as the night got darker and the noisy crickets got louder, Grannyma and Kaddy were taken up with finishing day duties and preparing for security and rest. Uncle made his way with a lantern around the structures in the yard, chasing poultry into pens and securing them. There were cows, goats and sheep all ready to go to sleep. After a while the three humans secured themselves upstairs and Grannyma laid out dinner. Kaddy ate fat heavy slices of home made bread with home made pineapple jelly and hot black lemon grass tea. It was deliciously Good! Uncle and Grannyma were talking about relatives and other family stuff. Kaddy cleared away dinner while Grannyma sat back in her rocking chair and Uncle lay on the sofa. Kaddy excused herself early and retired to the bedroom she had to share that night. She was tired. She had washed briefly with the cold water in the washing room and it made her sleepy. So much had happened. So much yet to understand. Kaddy got out her prayer rug and kneeled for her night prayers. She changed into a comfortable cool night gown and crawled under the mosquito net unto Grannyma's white cotton bed sheet. It was cozy. Kaddy pulled the covers up to her waist and relaxed on her back. "Thank you My Beautiful Creator for shelter this night," she said softly, "and please help me in my life ahead." "I am in your hands", she said as she looked up through the window, past the twinkling dots in the darkness. And poor Kaddy fell asleep. She did not feel Grannyma move her over to one side of the bed. She did not feel the aging hands pat her head and stroke her face. She didn't even feel the kiss on her forehead. Grannyma watched over the child that was brought back to her after seventeen years. She sat on her prayer rug beside the bed and spoke to the Almighty God. "Help Me!" she said as she cried into her cupped palms. "Please Help me my God to do right this time."

CHAPTER SIX

Feathers and Hooves and Lucy

Life in the Big Shop was busy but life with Big G, (as Kaddy referred to Grannyma,) was just something else. There was no line of customers waiting to be served but there were more eager moos and bleats and clucks waiting for nourishment from Grannyma's hand. It was a terrifying crowd. Kaddy had to learn fast or the 'pecky' ducks would eat her 'raw'. Very early, just past dawn, Big G was up, dressed and in her 'pens'. First it was the Big Guys. The sheep and goats and cows were unlocked and made to go to the pasture behind the house. Two long metal containers lay just beyond the gate to the wide rolling grassy fields. One was filled with clean water from a hose attached to a water pipe in the main yard. The other was filled with 'feed' from big bags stored in a wooden store house. Grannyma said that the 'feed' was extra nutrients aside from the fresh pasture grass for anyone who wanted it. When all of the thirty two four legged hungries were safely in the pasture, Big G would return to the pen to attend to Miss Lucy. She it seemed was 'family'. She was the Big white Cow reared by Grannyma from the time her mother died giving birth to her. Now she had already birthed three calves in three years. This was her third 'child'. It was milking time. She had been washed and left to dry. The teats were plump and ready. Big G called Kaddy close. Lucy turned the Big head on her four hundred and fifty pound body and looked with seeming disdain and superiority and nudged Grannyma as she sat on a small stool and placed a clean bucket under the bulging pink Lucy udders. Big G laughed. "It okay Lucy! Its okay." She told the concerned cow. Lucy gave a half moo. Big G laughed again. "This is Kaddy. She has come to live with us," Grannyma explained as her expert hands worked up and down like a twin lever machine pulling creamy warm milk into the big bucket. Soon they were done. Lucy was tied with a rope around her neck. Now Big G held the rope and walked the big white cow out of the pen and beyond the yard to the pasture plains. The rope was then taken off from her neck and she was allowed the freedom of fresh air and wide green land. Big G patted her head and Lucy mooed as she was let go. She ate from the 'feed' and drank clear clean water. She then mooed a low yet loud moo and a month old calf mooed back and left the grass she was nibbling to suck upon the chubby 'milk bottles' ready just for her. It was the Poultry Run next. On dry days they would be let out of the pens to scratch and fuzzle in the garden around them. On wet rainy days, they were given fresh feed in shiny hanging feeding cans and clean water. Kaddy was amused at the variety and needs and attributes of the 'yard' family. The "Setting hens", were the clucky fussy feathered ladies who watched over their straw nests of ten to fourteen eggs each. It was these eggs that some dogs liked to steal to eat. These eggs and forthcoming chicks would also attract snakes and other creatures who found them as easy prey. There was only one batch of already hatched chicks for Kaddy to see. The proud mother strutted about with eight four ounce golden feathered chickees. Then there were the Current Layers. These were hens who after daily fertilization rituals by Mr Rooster, would produce warm brown eggs unto straw beds. Grannyma would decide to 'pick up' some eggs every day or she would leave them under a hen who wanted to 'set' or 'sit'. The entire process was overlooked by Mr Rooster. A tall tailed multi colored gentleman he was with a rich red comb around his long hard sharp beak. He did his duty to his hens and proudly crowed when eggs fell into the nests. He liked to chase after the up coming females and showed off his maleness by flying unto fence posts and to the top of the pens. The hardest and most necessary part of the Operations was the Clean-up. All water and feeding pans had to be cleaned two times a day, for the morning and afternoon feeding. The hens needed special dry bedding of wood shavings or straw for the bottom of their pens. This had to be checked and cleared if it was too damp and messy. The hens had to be kept dry and clean or they would get sick. Kaddy was not new to hard work or cleaning but when faced with the overnight dung build up in the Big Guys pens she didn't think the potato and rats in the Big shop were so bad. After the Four legged stock were put to pasture, their pens had to be opened and washed out with water from a hose. All the stuff was washed into concrete drains that flowed to bigger drains behind the house.

Kaddy soon developed her own strategy of coping. As long as she had lots of water and cleaning agents she was happy to clean. She helped Big G with most of the work but she would not go near Lucy. Grannyma pleaded with Kaddy to sit on the stool and give it a try. There were three legs too many on Lucy and Kaddy could see herself being easily crushed under those heavy udders. If Lucy decided to kick in anger Big G had the built and size to be steady but not Kaddy. She could imagine those big hooves all over her thin frame. Lucy thought she was Grannyma's baby. Kaddy was intruding. Grannyma just let it be.

CHAPTER SEVEN

A Visit from Uncle

A nd so it was that Kaddy existed. There was a good part of the day when the Feathers And Hooves had been fed and the house was tidied and the food all ready that Kaddy had the hammock for herself. She would sit and push off with her feet as high as it could go and then lay back and enjoy the three or five minutes of sweet rocking sensation. It was relaxing and soothing. She now understood why babies liked to be rocked. Sometimes she would help Grannyma do the washing by hand in the Big plastic tub. There was soaking and scrubbing and rinsing and wringing and shaking and then pinning on the long lines in the drying sun. With tall items like sheets and towels Big G would use a long wooden stick to prop up the middle of the line so that the edges of the clean clothes would not touch the grass in the yard. Kaddy always had clothes to rewash because the birds thought the line was a nice pooping perch. After settling in for a month Uncle came to visit on a quiet Sunday. Kaddy was so glad to see his car pull up, she ran through the yard and gate and greeted him with a big hug. It felt so natural. Uncle laughed and hugged her and together they walked in. "Hi Sweetie", he said to her, "You look well and happy." Kaddy smiled and let him go as Grannyma came out to greet him. "So how are things here?" he asked. Big G laughed. "Oh good! She is helping me but she would not go anywhere near Lucy," she told Uncle. They all laughed and Kaddy went inside to get lemonade and cake for Uncle. Kaddy asked about aunt

Molly and Elizabeth. "They are both well." was all he said. He had come on some business with Grannyma. As they sat alone, while Big G went to get some private papers, Kaddy told Uncle she was happy to see him. He said he was happy she was settled and well. He then reached into his pocket and took out a roll of money and gave it to her. "You keep this child if there is any need. I promised your mother I would take care of you." "I am sorry about Lizze and your aunt", he said and sighed. Kaddy took the money and went to her room to put it safely away. She sat on her bed, a head full of thoughts until Grannyma called to say that Uncle was leaving. Kaddy hugged him tightly and told him she loved him and walked with him across the old bridge to his car. "Take care baby," he told her, "I miss you." She waved as he started the car and took off down the sandy trail. She felt sad after he left. At least someone missed her.

CHAPTER EIGHT

Rain and Trouble

L ife with Grannyma continued. Some days were lazy good when together they would make coconut cakes and bake red rolls with sweetened coconut couscous, or they would indulge in sweet coconut water and luscious white jelly from fresh picked coconuts. The land was populated with coconut trees. Coconuts were used for cooking and baking and making oil and eating. Kaddy made Sundays her Tree Climbing day. The biggest golden dunks were at the top of the solid prickly trees. The ripest mangoes were on the far away branches. The sweetest sapodillas were hidden between the thick leaves. On Grannyma's estate there were trees of every type of fruit. Shiny jellied ginips and tangy 'white lady' guavas and juicy tangerines, and pearly pomegranates, and sour tamarinds, and pink cashews and golden sumatoos . . . . There was always a fruit in 'season' and Kaddy picked and had her fill. Big G would show her to make jams or drink or some other delicacy with the fruits. Grannyma enjoyed the enthusiasm and youth of Kaddy. Together they passed the weeks of two years. One night after a quiet hot Sunday Kaddy fell asleep early and dreamt of her mother all night. She saw Maman sitting on Grannyma's bed and packing her trunk. Her Mama wore a blue dress and she had flowers in her hair. Kaddy awoke early. She could smell her Maman's perfume. "Oh Mama ", she said aloud, "I know you are here. I wish I can see you." Kaddy looked around the room. "How I miss you my Mama." She said through her tears. Maman was happy in the dream but that week was upside down for Kaddy. The Rains came heavily on Tuesday. It was very heavy rain with loud angry thunder and sharp vicious lightening. That usually meant hot soup and brownies and good stories cuddled up beside Maman but it was trouble at Grannyma's. Big G knew it would rain and the animals knew it too but some animals were stubborn and they had strayed far into the pasture. Big G had gone out to find them and she was still out when the thunderstorm began. It was only 2.30 in the afternoon but it was dark sweaty humid hot. Kaddy lit the lamps upstairs and prepared the tea. Grannyma had fried a chicken whole so that the meat could keep for a couple days. Kaddy found potatoes and carrots and shallots and she put on a pot of soup. Thank God, Grannyma had indulged in the luxury of a four burner gas stove. Poor G was somewhere out in the rain. She would need hot soup when she got home. It was more than an hour after before Grannyma's voice could be heard calling for Kaddy. Big G was soaked, tired and shaking. She stood in a large tub and let herself drip. Kaddy watched her shivering and knew she had to help. Somehow and not too gently the wet clothes came off, all of them. Then Kaddy wrapped Grannyma in her bathrobe, put the soft slippers for her feet and took her to sit in the rocking chair.

Grannyma was quiet. She lay back in the chair and closed her eyes. Kaddy spooned some hot soup into a deep bowl and took it to the shivering lady. She had ague. It was a state of shivering induced by fever or fear. Kaddy had seen her Maman with it. Kaddy rubbed Grannyma's hands together to get them warm. She rubbed her all over. She then tried to get Big G to swallow the hot soup. It worked. It warmed Grannyma from her lips all the way in. All this while there was no word from the old lady. Kaddy guided her to her room and helped her take off the damp robe and get dressed in a warm long nightgown. She dried her hair with a towel as she sat on the bed. Then Big G quietly asked for hot tea. Kaddy hurried to the kitchen. The shivering Grannyma took two tablets from a drawer in her dresser and drank all of the hot tea. Kaddy made her lie back on the bed and covered her with a thick blanket. She secured the mosquito net and left Big G to rest. The rainstorm continued outside. Kaddy went back to the kitchen to put away the food and check on the doors and windows. She took a bowl of soup with some bread. When all was secure she took her lantern to her room. It didn't seem right to leave Grannyma alone. Kaddy changed and went to Big G's room. She was snoring quietly but the ague perspiration was on her forehead. Kaddy hung the lantern safely, closed the door and got in under the net at the back of Big Grannyma. She got really close and snuggled in. It was a night to be warm. "Please God, Please let Grannyma be alright." Kaddy prayed. The thunder announced itself continuously and the lightening tried to peep through the thick curtains at the window. The two ladies didn't take heed.

Wednesday morning dawned. Big G was up first. She looked at the sleeping Kaddy and smiled. "Thank God for the child." Big G changed to go outside. She had to check on the animals. It was not good. Two coconut trees behind the pens had fallen and smashed the roof of the hen house. The door of the goat shed was open. The animals were all over. Water had come up in the drains to cover the wooden bridge and the low edges of the yard. Grannyma did not know what to begin clearing first. As she stood under the house with one hand on her hip, an old truck pulled up at the gate. An old Grandfather still chipper and light on his feet stepped out. He lifted his cap in respect and called out to Grannyma. "What you doing Maisy Rae", Kaddy heard someone call out as she came to find the Grandma. There was concern in the greeting but definite mischief too. Kaddy turned to look at the Stranger at the gate. "What you doing at my gate Mr Row?" Grannyma said to the gate. "Mr Row", well dressed in long boots and jacket and cap advanced through the water to open the gate to meet the ladies. He turned to an amused Kaddy and took off his cap. "Good Morning ladies and its Uncle Harry Row to you Sweet Thing," he said as he grabbed Kaddy's hand and shook it. Kaddy liked him. He tried to grab Grannyma's hand. "Hi Beautiful Maisy, its nice to see you alive this morning," he said to her face. "Cant say the same for some folk", Grannyma said and Harry Row laughed. "Look here Maisy. I know how stubborn you are but I had to come check up on you. We had a real fiery hurricane last night. Many animals are sick and many nice folks are stranded." Mr Row was explaining to Big G. He turned to Kaddy. "Glad you have such good company but I think you should come up to the House until the water dries up." Harry Row was saying. "We are just fine, Thank You Mr Row". Grannyma said to the gentleman. "Now you get busy saving real Needy Ones, we are just as well as you can see." Grannyma continued. Kaddy thought to herself, "Thank God he didn't see you last night Big G." "I know you would say that. You are still stubborn Maisy Rae but still beautiful," Mr Row said to Grannyma, and with the last phrase he made sure he was quickly over the watery bridge. "Take care now Sweet Missy", he tipped his cap to Kaddy and backed his truck away. "You don't go listening to anything that man has to say," Grannyma told Kaddy. Kaddy shrugged and smiled. Grannyma and Harry Row, there was a story there . . . . The rest of Wednesday was restless. Lucy's calf was missing. Grannyma allowed Lucy and whoeverelse wanted to stay to make home around the hammock. Some hens were already in there. Dung and poop mingled with the wetness of the earth. It was ugly outside. Even Big G accepted that there was not much that could be done until the waters dried up and the rains moved on. On Thursday Grannyma was sick again. There was more rain. They stayed indoors. On Friday Grannyma's fevers got worse. The painkillers did not work. The soup could not stay down. For most of the day Big G was delirious and weak. Kaddy had to get help. She tried to talk to the sick old lady. Kaddy prayed and cried. She was afraid. Then sometime in the afternoon Grannyma grabbed Kaddy's arm and said to her ear, "Go to the Mansion. Go to the Mansion. Go get Harry." Then Grannyma became unconscious. Kaddy did not know what to do. Water was all around the yard. The old bridge was totally submerged. She did not know where to find the Mansion or Mr Harry Row. She had to leave Big G alone but she had to do something to save her. Kaddy put on her coat and long boots and made her way downstairs past the sheltering poultry and cattle and to the watery bridge. She looked up to the still dark sky and prayed. "Dear God, Please Guide me where to go. Grannyma needs help. Please show me the way." She then stepped unto the old bridge under two feet of water and cautiously took firm steps across to the road. It was yucky and slippery but Kaddy made it over the bridge to the high red road. She walked in the direction Harry's truck had come. Animals lay dead on the side of the road. Kaddy kept walking but saw no one. She was alone on a lonely road. "You are never alone baby." Mama used to say that. It was getting darker. Kaddy wanted to go back, and then she heard the sound of something. She looked ahead and waved her arms over her head. It was Harry Row in his truck. He pulled up near and opened the door so she could get in. Kaddy started to cry. It was a despairing, being scared, thankful cry. "Grannyma is sick, please hurry," she told Mr Row. He patted her cold fingers and drove quickly in silence to Grannyma's gate. Big G was worse. She was mumbling and calling names. She called for Kaddy and then she was asking for Haley. Why Kaddy wondered would Grannyma call the name of Kaddy's mother in her fevers. Kaddy packed clean clothes for both of them and she helped Harry Row dress Grannyma in warm clothes. He lifted the sick lady down the stairs and across the watery bridge and into the front seat of his truck. Kaddy secured the front door and looked around. Lucy stood by in a foot of water. She looked at Harry Row putting Grannyma into the truck and she mooed. Kaddy spoke to the cow. "We have to leave. She is sick," Kaddy said to Lucy. Lucy mooed again. Kaddy made her way across the bridge and into the truck. She sat at the other end with Grannyma in the middle and held the sick lady close so Harry Row could drive.

CHAPTER NINE

Kaddy at the Mansion

It took about one hour. Harry Row pulled into a long driveway of a private estate and the Mansion. It was huge and impressive. It was a long three storey block of a house, stately, pretty and warm. There were stairs everywhere, long polished wooden stairs that turned corners and took you from one floor to the other. Harry Row held Grannyma like a baby up two sets of stairs to a bedroom on the first floor. He flicked a switch by the door with his chin and soft yellow glow lit up a comfortable four poster bed. Past the high dresser and vanity and Queen Ann bench, lay modern toilet facilities and bath. Grannyma was laid gently on the bed. Harry Row insisted that Kaddy take her own room similarily finished, but for tonight, Kaddy wanted to be close to Grannyma. Mr Row left and Kaddy could hear him giving instructions downstairs. He had taken off the cap, jacket and boots and soon returned in soft shoes and short sleeved shirt. Handsome man, Kaddy thought, even with his silvering head. He came into the room holding a Doctor's bag. "I am a doctor, a medical practitioner," he said to Kaddy as he sat on the bed next to sick Grannyma. "I have my own clinic here in this building and a complete Laboratory. I asked the Nurse to stay on so we can attend to patients who come in the night." As he explained, a bright looking motherly lady came into the room and proceeded to put up the sleeves of Grannyma's gown so that her blood pressure could be checked. Kaddy was exhausted. "You can get cleaned up in your room", Harry

Row said to her without lifting his head from the BP monitor. Kaddy did not want to be ungrateful to Grannyma but it was Doctor's Orders or suggestion . . . . She took her things into the next room. Everything was done in a light shade of pink. It was sooo pretty, the wall paper, the curtains, the bed curtains, the bedside lamp shades, the cushions, the bathroom tiles. Kaddy loved the bathroom. The water was both hot and cold. She set the control knobs just right and stood under the shower. She missed a shower. The water warmed all over. She lathered with fresh botanicals bath foam and felt clean and pretty. She shampooed and conditioned her hair and put on a clean night shirt. Kaddy sat in front of the vanity mirror and brushed the wet hair. There was a hair dryer on the wall and she sat in comfort and blow dried her hair. Bathing and grooming made her tired. She decided to lay on the cool cotton sheets of the King sized bed to relax for a few minutes. It was almost midnight, about four hours after, when Kaddy awoke. Strangeness anchored her movements until she remembered the day's events. Grannyma!

Kaddy had abandoned the poor sick woman. She quickly slipped her robe on, put on the soft slippers she found at the side of the bed and opened the door quietly. There was no noise down the hall. Kaddy pushed the door of Grannyma's room. It opened slowly. The room was lit by the soft hues of a hand painted rose patterned bedside lamp. As she walked to the bed, she heard someone clear his throat. Dr Harry Row lay in a recliner beside the bed. Kaddy pulled back and he raised himself up to sit and motioned for her to come forward. Grannyma lay sleeping. Her bed was set up like a hospital bed. She had needles in her veins hooked to tubes and bags of solution and medicine hanging from metal holders. Dr Harry got up and whispered to Kaddy to follow him out of the room. "Your Grannyma needs to rest", he said. "She has Leptospirosis which she probably got from the animals in the flood waters. I have given her some special antibiotics. A nurse will check on her throughout the night." Kaddy listened as the doctor talked. "Thank you", Kaddy said. "Thank you for everything." "The room is very comfortable," Kaddy told the Doc. He smiled "Glad someone could use them", he said. "Are you hungry?" he asked her. "I can call Delia to get you something." Kaddy was very hungry but the thought of waking someone up to get her food was terrible. "No! No!" she protested, "I am very hungry but if you show me to the kitchen, I can manage." "Well, as you wish", and the good Doctor Uncle Row took Kaddy by the arm past corners and stairs and corridors and rooms to a huge White Kitchen. After making sure that she could find her way back to her room he left her to investigate. The Row Kitchen was like a mini supermarket. Kaddy opened the doors of the huge white refrigerator. She could see platters of baked chicken and potato salad and baked macaroni and cheese. There was cold fruit salad and a bowl of garden salad. The freezer had two long shelves with all the flavors of ice cream. The cupboards around the kitchen housed boxes and cans and jars of anything that could be eaten or used in a meal. This was not the time to discover all the treasures of Dr Harry Row's Kitchen. Kaddy got a clean plate and put heaping portions of creamy potato salad and cheesy macaroni on one side. She broke off the huge leg of the chicken and added that to the plate. She put the plate to warm up in the white roomy microwave. She took some juice and a good serving of chocolate ice cream and sat herself at the small table in the kitchen. She looked up to a wide screen television. Why Not? She thought. Between mouthfuls she searched the channels using the tv remote control. There were so many channels. Dr Harry was living the good life. Kaddy found reruns of 'Friends' and she sat back to enjoy. She cleaned up her plate and licked the spoon. It was all delicious. Years of practice made her wash and tidy up. She took the TV off and turned off the lights. She made her way back to Grannyma's room. The door was slightly open and Dr Row was again asleep in the recliner. There was a good story there Kaddy thought. He obviously loved Grannyma, his Maisy Rae. Kaddy tiptoed to her own room and closed the door. She brushed her teeth and got ready for bed. Everything was clean, safe and classy. The room was air conditioned and she did not need a net. There were no mosquitoes at the Mansion. Kaddy stood at the foot of the bed and allowed her body to fall into bed. She pummeled the soft pillows until she felt ready and in the right position for sleep. She lay under the covers and looked up to the pretty canopy of the bed. "Dear God", she said, "This is like being in a fancy hotel, not that I have ever been in one but I have seen them in movies. Thank You for all This. I don't know what happens next but please watch over us and take us to tomorrow."

CHAPTER TEN

A Story is Told

A lazy stretch and a wide yawn at 9.00am were suddenly stopped by a small voice. "Morning Miss Kaddy, do you want your breakfast now?" Kaddy laughed. "I am Miss Delia", the voice said as a pleasant thin lady stepped into view. Kaddy sat up in the bed. "Thank You Miss Delia, but it is okay. I will come down." The pleasant Miss Delia smiled. Kaddy made her way to the bathroom. She took her time, saturating, enduring, enjoying. The bathroom was big. There was a two seater sofa and a closet with clothes. There was a phone and television and a view to the garden downstairs. When Kaddy finally emerged from the bath, her own clothes were neatly ironed and laid out for her. The curtains were pulled back and the bed was made. Everything was neat and clean and Miss Delia was done and gone. It was already late so Kaddy quickly got dressed and went to check on Grannyma.

She was sitting up in her bed. The tubes and needles were gone but she still looked pale. "Good Morning Grannyma", Kaddy said as she walked in. They were alone. "Morning yourself, I wondered what happened to you", Grannyma said to the bright face. "I am sorry I slept so late," Kaddy said quietly, but Grannyma, you should see these rooms. This house is like a Royal Palace with maids and cleaners and even a House Doctor and Clinic and everything." Grannyma smiled at the bubbling in the child. "Come here Kaddy", she said, "I have to talk to you." Kaddy climbed unto the end of the huge bed and curled her feet under her. "What is it Grannyma?" she asked. There was a loud rap at the door and it was pushed open. A mature woman in a white apron approached the bed. "What you doing Ms Row? What sick you go get now?" the fussy apron said. She moved to Grannyma, adjusting her pillows behind her back, pulling her eyelids down, feeling her neck for a temperature. "Now you know you aint no young thing anymore. Its no use running. That man is lonely and he getting old on me", the apron continued, "Did you get your medicine yet? You want me to get some herbs from the garden?" "No! No! Martha, I am fine now. The Doc is looking after me." Grannyma was saying. Miss Martha still fussed, pushing the already drawn curtains a little further back and 'beating' the cushions on the Queen Anne sofa all the while muttering to herself. "You think you are some Farmhouse Queen, going to live with all those creatures. Woman don't know her place. You lucky that man wait for you." Grannyma said in a stern voice, "That is enough Martha! He is lucky I am here now!" "From what I hear, someone had to be carried up the stairs," Miss Martha still muttered in motherly 'Telling it like it is' fashion, as she rearranged the items on the vanity. "Well, sure hope all will be well now," Miss Martha said to the bed with her hand on her hips and pointing her right hand index finger to Grannyma she said, "you call me if you need anything." The white apron cast a glance to tiny Miss Kaddy and left the room. Kaddy uncurled her legs and walked to the windows and back. "Don't pay any attention to Miss Martha. She didn't mean to ignore you. She is really concerned about me", Grannyma was saying. Kaddy leaned against the window looking at Grannyma. Kaddy was not annoyed with Miss Martha. She was glad she was ignored. It was the norm for her and she did not feel she was deliberately avoided. The only words she got out of the conversation were "Ms Row". She repeated them to Grannyma. "Ms Row! As in Mistress of the Mansion, as in Wife to Dr Harry Row!" she asked Grannyma. Big G smiled coyly and said to Kaddy, "Come sit here child, there are things you have to know." As Kaddy sat once again on the bed, Grannyma continued quietly. "I know I could have died yesterday and you need to know your place in all of this." 'She had a place in all of this.' Kaddy thought about that sentence. "My name is Maisy Rae Row and the Doc and I got married in April thirty five years ago. I was twenty five and he was thirty. Martha started working here when I was expecting my son. She helped me through the hard delivery right here at this house. My beautiful Michael was born on a rainy night. But my baby got sick the next day and he could not breathe. Doc tried and tried but God took Michael back." Tears flowed down Granny Maisey's cheeks. Kaddy never thought the old lady could cry. Kaddy began to seriously listen to the tale. "I did not know how to live from day to day with empty arms," Grannyma said. "I did not want to leave the room." "Look out that window under the tallest palm tree," Grannyma told Kaddy. "Doc put our baby there." Kaddy went to the window and looked out unto the grounds of the Row Mansion. She saw the tall palm with baby roses at its root. After more than thirty years, Granny Maisey spoke as if it were yesterday. As Kaddy watched, she heard more. "One day Doc brought home the prettiest baby girl." Her mother had died giving birth to her and she had no relatives to care for her. "She was a noisy thing." Ms Row was smiling now as she remembered. "She took over the Mansion. Our days flew into years and she blossomed into a beautiful flower." Kaddy turned away from the window as Grannyma paused. Her voice changed to a sad, angry, 'Let Me tell it and get it over with' tone. "My beautiful daughter wanted to go study in the Capital. Harry was happy. She wanted to be a Doctor too. She was bright and smart and so sweet at seventeen." Grannny Maisey looked down at her hands and knew she had to tell all of the story. "In the first year after Winter break, my girl came home. She was different.

I thought she was tired. I bought her vitamins. I took her shopping. I made her rest. But she was in love and pregnant." Kaddy was astounded. "What!" She didn't know she said the word out aloud. Ms Row made a wry laugh and shook her head. "Losing Michael was terrible but seeing my baby girl's bulging tummy was a sickening gut wrenching experience. I was Angry, so angry. I barely spoke to her. She did not go back to College but stayed here and then that 'despicable creature' came." Grannyma was wringing her hands in the anguish of reliving painful memories. "They were in Love, he said. He pleaded for the sake of family and the child. But nothing made it any easier. All I could see was how he had soiled my child. "He wanted to marry her." Big G said with derision. "He was nineteen, she was eighteen. What could he give her? He was an artist. How good did he think he was?

"He was Good Maisey." Dr Harry Row entered the room and sat beside his wife on the bed holding her hands. She tried to pull away but he held them together in his. He had been listening to the story and Kaddy could see that tears were already wiped from his tired eyes. He opened his arm to Kaddy beckoning her to come to him. She moved and he hugged her and kissed her head. "What was that for?" she wondered. She eased herself out of the embrace and looked at Mr and Ms Row. Dr Harry bent his head to his Maisey and asked her gently, "Do you want me to tell some of the story?"

She shrugged. "You did a lot of mischief. Let me hear you say it." Doc did not care about her tone. He started his journey to times past. "If you could see them together Maisey, that boy loved our girl and she loved him and they were excited about that baby so I did the only proper thing there was to do. I took them to Pastor and got them married. It was a beautiful Sunday. Pastor's wife dressed the little chapel and Martha brought your wedding dress." Maisey Row turned her head sharply to Doc. "Martha did What!" Doc chuckled. "Yes Sweet Maisey, your daughter got married in your wedding dress." "Anyway", Doc wanted to continue. "Very soon it was time for the baby and you remember that Friday morning before the roosters crowed, our home heard the cries of another strong baby girl." "I remember everything about her", Granny Maisey smiled. "I was her mother for two whole years."

Doc turned to Kaddy. "It was the only way Maisey would make peace with everything. She looked after the baby while the young parents went back to College and their life of love. The young man was having his first Art Show. Our girl would not leave him." Then Doc stopped speaking. GrannyMaisey was quiet too. The silence went on for a long minute. Kaddy asked, "What happened?" They both sighed. Dr Harry spoke up. "The Art Show was a success. They were coming home for the Baby's second birthday .... and there was an accident. The artist was driving and he died in an instant on impact. We pulled our daughter from the wreck. She kept calling his name. Nothing was ever the same again."

Doc looked over at Maisey and they were quiet again. Kaddy was crying. She felt a stirring in her heart and she could not stop the tears. Even her feet felt weak and wobbly. She did not understand her own emotion. She sat on the Queen Anne bench facing them. "How am I a part of all this Uncle Harry?" Kaddy asked. Doc continued his tale. "The young man who died that day", Doc paused, "His name was Andrew." "The young woman, our beautiful daughter who we nursed back to health, her name was Haley. The baby we kept for two years, we named her Maryam." Dr Harry wanted to tell the whole story and Kaddy listened. "Two months after the accident Haley decided to leave. She did not want to stay in a home that did not love her Andrew. I saw her open the doors to go out with Maryam. That baby was all she had of Andrew. They were leaving together."

Granny Maisey Row was crying again. "You took them away from me," she said. Doc sighed and got up from the bed to face the window. "She was leaving Maisey! I could not stop her! She was hurting terribly Maisey. She was leaving with Maryam." "I told her I would take her to a good place", Doc said. "I drove them to old Uncle Seth's house." Grannyma continued the narrative. "I left that day too. I could not live with you anymore. You had taken both of my children away from me." "You never gave me a chance to explain Maisey," Doc said quietly.

Granny Maisey turned to Kaddy and told her, "I packed up and went to live in my Grandmother's Farmhouse." "You left Here to go live in that Farmhouse for the past seventeen years!" It was a statement from Kaddy. "Anger and misunderstanding can make that happen", Ms Maisey Row said. Then she looked up at Kaddy's face and said to the listening young lady, "Kaddy, do you understand anything we have been saying to you?" So much had been said. It was a sad long story. Maybe she missed something, Kaddy thought. "Come here child", Grannyma said very gently. Kaddy stood in front of her. "You look very much like your mother." Grannyma said. "Don't you know you are our Maryam. Your father's name was Andrew. Your mother's name was Haley." "Andrew loves Haley", the words on the cardboard heart card her mother had left . . . .

"What!" Kaddy exclaimed. "My Mother, was your Haley?" The silence from both of them answered her. "You, are my Grandmother and you are my Grandfather and I was born in this house!" More silence to her words. "So why did I not see you before? Why did I have to go live with Uncle and Aunt Molly? Why did I live only with my mother for ten years? Why only Uncle and I were there when she was buried? The questions poured out of Kaddy and she sat on the carpet on the floor and put her face in her hands. Her lonely Maman had no one. Kaddy let the tears fall warm and salty down her cheeks. Doc sat flat on the carpet and held Kaddy to him. She tried to be stubborn but wandering and loneliness had made her mellow. She leaned back into the arms of her Grandfather.

He stroked her hair and lay his head against hers. "No more crying, my baby girl', he said to her. After a couple minutes when it was all quiet, Doc spoke again. "The same day I took you and your mama to Uncle Seth's house, I returned to find Maisey gone. I went back to Haley to ask her to come back home but instead she took you and went away where we could not find her." "Somehow, she found the village of her Birth Mother who had left an older son, that is your Uncle Raymond." "That was a very difficult year". Grandfather Row was saying . . . . I was ill after Maisey left but I did not stop looking for you and your mom." "When I did find the place I had to deal with Raymond." "He was a proud young man. He had promised your Mama that he would take care of the two of you. Haley did not want to leave him either. She had found a brother."

Kaddy listened quietly as the head above hers told the story. "Raymond was already married with an eight year old daughter but he made sure that you and mama had enough to eat and live on. His wife was a fiery tempered girl who refused to have you and Haley live with her in the same house. Your Uncle rented a one bedroom apartment and you and mama were happy there." "You knew where we were?" Kaddy asked from under his chin. "I knew what your Uncle Raymond said. You were safe and well. He said I was not to be a part of your lives. Your mama wanted it that way." "I let Raymond know that he could come to me for anything he needed but he never did." "That is because you live in this Mansion," Big G said with a short laugh. "Raymond would not take help."

"So what did You do all this time Grannyma "? Kaddy asked in as serious a tone as a nineteen year old under a Grandfather's chin could sound. "Don't go using that tone with me young lady," Grannyma said. "Who do you think has been paying your school and examination fees?" Did you really think Molly Whats Her Name would let her husband pay for you to go to the same school as her precious Elizabeth?" Doc Harry let Kaddy out of his hug and stared at Ms Maisey Row. "You knew where she was?" "Haley was angry for all of us." Grannyma said. "She did not want us in her life anymore and especially not in yours," she addressed Kaddy. "But I found Raymond and he came to visit many times. I insisted that I wanted to pay for your schooling and he accepted because it was not easy taking money out of his business with that wife of his. I gave him money to take your mama to a good doctor but your mama did not care to live after your daddy died." "Haley was not well since the accident. Raymond told me she got chills and fevers a lot." "But you did not come to her funeral! You did not come for me!" Kaddy cried out and she got up and folded her arms and leaned against the window. "That was your Uncle's decision", Big G made it clear. "He was so distraught. He could not let you go with anyone else. It was his duty he said to his sister. He thought it was best we did not go to the funeral." "We buried her in a beautiful garden where Maman said Daddy is buried too," Kaddy added softly. "I know", Grannyma said. "I have been there many times." Doc Harry was listening to the ladies and then he stood up and waved his right index finger in the air. "Well, You Both have that wrong," he said with a smile. Kaddy turned to him. "What do you mean Grandfather?"

CHAPTER ELEVEN

Lucy at the Mansion

Delia came running up the stairs shouting. "Ms Row! Doc! Ms Row! Doc! He eating all the daisies and flowers and everything. We can't stop him! Please come! The Garden!" And Delia the young maid went to the window wringing her hands. Doc and Kaddy looked out the window to the Garden below. "What is happening down there?" they asked Delia. "Its a Cow Doc! A Big Big Cow!" Delia was so upset. She turned to go back downstairs and Doc followed her. Grannyma was laughing. "I am sure its Lucy. That girl has come looking for me. Kaddy help me get down these stairs."

Sure enough, it was Lucy, the four hundred and fifty pound Cow from the Farmhouse. She had trampled all through the front Gardens and she had Doc and Delia running behind her. The Landscape was truly thrashed. How GrannyMaisey laughed. She stood on the low porch and laughed. Lucy heard her and stopped. Then she cantered up to the porch and mooed. Grannyma put out her hand and touched Lucy's head. Lucy mooed some more. "You Big Baby!" Grandma said to her as Delia and Doc panted to a stop. "How did she get here?" young Delia wanted to know. "It is Love, child, just Love." Big G said. Lucy climbed unto the low porch and sat down right next to Grannyma's feet. It was the strangest sight to see a huge white cow lying on her side with her Big Head against Grannyma's feet. Big G talked to her, stroked her, asked her about her calf and pacified her with loving expressions of how she had lost weight and must be hungry.

Kaddy had climbed unto the rails of the porch when she saw Lucy going to Grandma Maisey. She still stood high and away from the tired cow. Doc looked on at his Not too long ago Sick Wife touching the dirty wandering cow. He told his wife, "Well! She cant stay here Maisey. I will put her in the garage at the back." And so it was that Lucy the Big Cow from the Farmhouse, joined the family at the Mansion. Doc Harry helped Kaddy down and instructed her to take Ms Row back to her room. The Nurse was there to check her and get her medicine. Kaddy kissed her Grandma and went to her own room.

Kaddy lay on her bed totally spent and fatigued. It was almost lunch time but she had had no breakfast. She was feeling light headed but it was not because she needed food. All the years, all this time, she thought she had no one. She was the Orphan Girl, the girl who wore Lizzie's Hand me Downs and Lizzie's old shoes, the girl who cleaned, the girl who stayed Out of Sight . . . . Now she had Grandma Maisey Row and Grandfather Doctor Harry Row and Delia and Martha and a Mansion . . . . Her Daddy was an artist. Her mama and daddy loved each other and she was a child of their love. Kaddy was calm with thanks and humility. She sat beside her bed and looked to the blue sky and sunshine through her window. "Most Beautiful Creator, How Bountiful are thy Favors," she said. "Never make me Greedy or Ungrateful but help me to Please you more each day."

CHAPTER TWELVE

Life goes on at the Mansion

For the rest of the week Grandma Maisey tried getting stronger. Doc Harry would take her outside and they would talk and talk and even nap outside under the beautiful shady boughs or in the fancy gazebos. Kaddy looked out from her bedroom window at the couple in love. Kaddy thought often about That Night at aunt Molly's. It was so horrible. How could she spill the fruit. What a mess it was. But He looked at her . . . . and He touched her hand. Something ran like an electric current through her nerve centers and it made her feel warm and hot at the same time. She remembered his voice, so caring and firm yet soft, "Let me help you," he said. She could remember his eyes, black like a velvet purse. Where did he go, she wondered. Did he feel anything like she felt that night? Kaddy got up and walked to the vanity mirror. She was not so bad looking. She did look really nice sometimes. She remembered the Peach Dress she wore that night. Did he think she looked nice that night? Kaddy got up and looked out of the window again. Grandpa had leaned over hot Grandma Maisey and he was kissing her. She was sixty. He was sixtyfive. They were apart for seventeen years and now they were kissing and they didn't care who looked. It would be nice to be kissed, Kaddy thought, but it only mattered if both people were in love. Kaddy shook the thoughts away. She had to wait for her Life's Chart to unroll.

After a while Grandma Maisey was strong and well again. She tried to replant the front Gardens that Ms Lucy had so quickly undone.

Lucy was sent to a Gentleman farmer with a huge pasture on high land and modern feeding and milking facilities. Uncle came up one weekend and he and some workers went over to the Farmhouse. They recovered some faithful hens and goats but many of the animals had wandered far into the farmlands or were lying dead. Those recovered were given to small farmers in the village. Grannyma told Uncle that she had transferred ownership of the Farm to him and she insisted that he should take it. They all decided that it was best to sell the Old place. Kaddy enjoyed the privileged life at the Mansion. She worked many days as Grandpa's Assistant in his Clinic learning whatever he could teach about helping sick people.

She helped to deliver many babies, she helped to circumcise little tingies, she dressed wounds and stitched cuts and gave lollipops to scared little ones. Soon a year had gone by. Kaddy found a room full of treasure on the upper flat. It was the room where Haley and Andrew spent their time nurturing their love in Haley's womb. Kaddy's Dad's artwork was all over the room. He was good. He had sketched Mama in all poses with and without clothes. He had also done Kaddy as a baby, crying, suckling at her mother, sleeping, laughing . . . They had named her Maryam. Mama had changed it to Kaddy. Kaddy like both names. She would like to be called Miss Maryam Kaddy . . . One day on a clear cool Sunday Grandpa called Kaddy and Grandma Maisey and told them that he had to show them both something. He took them to a beautiful garden at the back of the house. It was fenced with a hedge of yellow rose bushes. Inside the yellow hedge were formations of blood red roses and the whitest white scented lilies. There was a little white picket gate to open to enter the peaceful, beautiful sanctuary. Grandma was so excited to know what lay beyond the fence. Doc Harry held both of them on either arm and spoke quietly and clearly. "I said once to both of you that you did not have all the facts about the past. I could not interfere in my daughter's life while she was alive but I tried to put things right after death." He unhooked the little white gate and took them through the Garden. There in two earthy mounds lay the remains of Andrew and Haley Wills. Grandpa had gotten permission to bring his daughter and her love to rest together at home. Grandma Maisey held on to Kaddy and sobbed. The pain of love and separation and death would not go away. Kaddy was very happy her parents were together at the Mansion once again. Grandpa Row had arranged for the Pastor who had married Andrew and Haley to come by. In a crying ceremony the two loves were sent prayers and good wishes to continue the Good Sleep. Grandma and Kaddy visited the Garden often. "I am sorry Andrew." "I am sorry Haley", she said one day but most of the time she spoke to Haley. She told her Andrew was Good and he could paint well. Kaddy learned early to Forgive from Maman and not to have bad thoughts about people. She was sorry Maman was not able to do that when she was alive.

CHAPTER THIRTEEN

Questions and Answers

As Spring came in the New Year, Uncle Raymond brought good news.

Elizabeth was getting married. She had bagged a rich lawyer, many years older but who cared, he doted on fair Lizzie. Uncle seemed relieved. Aunt Molly was calling caterers and checking on halls and ordering dresses. The good Lawyer was once married but his wife died early without having any children. He was successfully established in the Big Country. Lizzie was going to live in the Big Country. As Grandma Maisey and Grandpa Harry listened, Grandma made a suggestion. "Raymond, you don't have to spend anything. Have the wedding here." Grandpa quickly agreed and the more he thought about it the happier he was. "Sure, Sure. we have all the space here and all the facilities. It has been so long since we had a celebration. These grounds need some festivity." Grandpa assured Uncle. Raymond was happy but he was not so sure about Molly. It so happens she was so happy she didn't fuss and when she heard that it was free she was ecstatic at her savings. Now she could concentrate on the dress, the cake and the wedding favors. When the Good Lawyer said he was bringing the dress from the Big Country, Molly turned to Mush. She was the luckiest Mother-in-law. The marriage was truly Blessed. And so it was that life at the Mansion got busier. Gardens were prepped and hedges were trimmed and gazebos were repainted . . . the place was all 'spruced up'. There was going to be a Wedding at the Mansion. It made everyone happier to be a part of the cleaning and arranging and polishing.

It was one week before Lizzie's Day. Uncle had come to check on seating and placements and whatever else was needed. Kaddy was happy for Lizzie but she had some questions and she wanted to ask her uncle. She caught up with him in one of the gazebo gardens as he relaxed from the hot sun. "Hi there Pet!" he said to her. "Whats up?" "Uncle can I ask you about something," Lizzie said as she sat next to him on the bench. "Sure Sweetie. What is it?" Uncle asked. Kaddy had wondered about it so often, she had no hesitation with the words now. "Uncle, why did Aunt Molly ask you to take me away?" "Oh That!" Uncle said as he sat up from his relaxed posture. "Aunt Molly was angry child," "What did I do?" Kaddy asked again. "It wasn't you Kaddy, its that boy, that Andy boy." Uncle said reluctantly. "What did he do?" Kaddy persisted. "Well!" Uncle rubbed the back of his neck. "Its what he didn't do. He said he didn't want to marry Lizzie." "He said he was in love with someone else." Uncle gave the information because he was asked. "Well!" Kaddy thought quickly, "I am sure you are glad how things worked out." "Aunt Molly prefers this lawyer for Lizzie, Right?" "Yes! Yes! Sure! Harold is a fine young man." Uncle said smiling. "I am sure Aunt Molly has forgotten about that Andy boy now." Kaddy said quietly. Uncle dismissed that whole issue and agreed with her with a wave of his hand. Kaddy allowed some minutes to pass then she asked again. "But why did she have to chase me away?" "I don't understand Uncle."

Uncle Raymond realized that it was due. Kaddy needed an explanation. Still rubbing the back of his neck, he took his time with the words. He gripped the bench with both hands and looked to the floor of the gazebo as he spoke. "If you remember Kaddy, Andy's mother came to visit. She told us she was upset with her son. Andy told his mother that he had fallen in love with you and you were the only girl he would marry." "I told them that you were too young but Molly would not encourage it." "To have that boy come to see Lizzie and choose you! Molly could not have you in the same house anymore."

"So! So! What happened to him?" Kaddy stammered. "He left to go to the Big Country", Uncle said. "They are coming for the wedding." "Molly wants him to see Lizzie happy and married." With that last update uncle got up. He gave Kaddy a hug and told her, "I have to go now babe." "You take care and don't worry yourself with things of the past." Kaddy smiled and watched him leave in a hurry. Kaddy was smiling and smiling. Andy told everyone he loved her. He loved her and he wanted to marry her. Uncle didn't think that he was serious. Uncle never even considered Kaddy getting married. He still saw her as his little niece. Kaddy was growing up. She had just passed her twentieth birthday.

Kaddy was happy. Andy said he loved her, the fruit girl, the orphan girl. She skipped through all the gardens and into the kitchen and up the stairs into her room. Three years had gone by. Andy had left for far shores. There may have been pretty girls but Kaddy had hope. He was coming to the Mansion. He was going to be there in a week. It was a crazy hope to build on a Touch but Kaddy was in love.

With three days to go, Aunt Molly and Lizzie and Uncle and their support team moved into the West wing of the Mansion. Kaddy did not let their coming dampen her happy mood. She hugged them and they hugged back and then they were off on their own business. Grandma Maisey had put them in the farthest part of the Mansion where they had their own way out and in and their private kitchen and staff. Although Kaddy had never given bad details about her stay in the Big Shop, her Grandma understood well the situation. But it was Martha who noticed the Glow in Kaddy's cheeks. Since she had come to know that Kaddy was Haley's girl, Martha had a jello heart for the child. She seemed to want to make up for the unhappiness and unpleasantness that had happened. "What has put the perk in your pansies?" Martha asked Kaddy as they both worked in the kitchen one day. Kaddy did not understand most of Martha's analogies but she understood the question. "Just the wedding preparations", Kaddy said mischievously as she took an apple from the fruit bowl and munched away. "Ah Ha!" Martha said, "and I am the Queen of Spain!" "You could be!" Kaddy laughed. "Just go over there, knock out the guards and declare yourself, Queen Martha of Spain." "Life isn't that easy Pumkin", Martha said quietly as she busied herself with separating the leaves on a large head of cabbage. Martha continued without looking up from her cabbage. "God is always in charge Babygirl. Sometimes His plan takes time to come together and sometimes He works very quickly." "It is all up to Him." "But whatever happens it is for the best for He is the Best of Planners." Martha then looked into the face of the apple chewing gums, and told her, "When we say we believe in God we have to accept His decisions about things in our life." Kaddy listened without interrupting. "I know all that", she said as she threw the apple kernel into the kitchen trash and joined Martha at the small table in the kitchen. "So whats up with you?" Martha asked again. Kaddy looked at the kind face of the Housekeeper. There was so much love at the Mansion with people who really cared about her. She needed to tell someone so she told Martha Everything . . . . She told about the Big Shop, Aunt Molly, Andy, the fruit bowl, everything. Martha had seen and heard a lot in her life and she knew more about bad endings than good ones. Of all the people in the world she did not want this child having wrong hopes. How could she warn her and not crush her at the same time. Martha's thoughts were busy. She needed collaboration on this matter. They had to wait until she met this Andy but before that she knew she had to talk to Ms Row. Maisey needed to know. Kaddy was waiting for a response. "What should I do?" she asked.

"Kaddy, you must pray special about this," Martha said to the blushing cheeks of the twenty year old. "Meanwhile," Martha asked as she took her bowl to the sink, "Do you know what you are going to wear? Did Lizzie ask you to be a Bridesmaid?"

"No! I was not asked and I am happy!" Kaddy said. "I prefer to freely mingle and observe the operations." Martha acted shocked as a fussy hen with a 'Slow to come out of her shell chick.' "None of that You!" Martha said. "We have to get you well groomed and dressed. You must go see Ms Pearl tomorrow." "Who is going into Town tomorrow?" Grandma Maisey asked as she walked into the kitchen. "This child has nothing to wear", Martha let her know. "She has to go see Pearl." "Sure", Big G said shaking her head. "I need some new things too." "You need new everything," Martha laughed. "You still have farmhouse smell on your skin." "Martha! Stop that!" Maisey told the chuckling cook. "I do need some professional grooming." Maisey agreed.

"And now you have the Doc checking." Martha quipped. "Keep in line Misses. Doc is your man girl. Keep him hopping." They all laughed and Kaddy left the Two Matures in their respectful companionship. She sought the privacy of her room. There was Hope and Fear in Kaddy's nervous heart. What if he did not remember her. What if he ignored her. Mama's blood group was B positive so she used to tell Kaddy, "Be positive child. Be positive." "If you want something bad enough, the angels are with you and the Great One may call it your way." Kaddy looked up at the sky through her bedroom window. "Its always up to You", she said. "Please help me God, Please."

CHAPTER FOURTEEN

A Visit to Pearl

Pearl's Shop was a pampering heaven. She in her curly wig and chunky pearls and jewel studded glasses and three quartered length dress with wayward scarf, did not promote the Vogue of the times but she knew how to cut, fluff and style and get a body stimulated and cleaned and dressed for a King's Ball.

She was proud of her crew of six belles, Sharon, Penelope, Suzy, Heather, Ariel and the most hard working sought after belle, Toni. He was the new acquisition. He could cut and fluff for any age and the ladies mooned over his head massage. Ms Pearl hugged him and kissed his cheek as she introduced him to Ms Row.

"Maisey Darling, my belle here would take good care of you", she said to Grandma as she plunked her in a cushy armchair. Then Pearl looked over her jeweled rims and inspected Kaddy. She walked around her and then addressed Martha. "Well! Well! What is this? Freshness! Bloom! Darling eyes! Kissing lips! My My! This one I do myself. Pearl will make you a Princess today." Kaddy was a canvas for their landscaping. She had never been to a Beauty Shop before. No one had ever 'attended to her' before. She was a little afraid but she had to trust them. She lay back in the comfortable chair and closed her eyes. Professional hands soaked her feet and scrubbed them and buffed them and shaped her nails and made them shine. The same was done to her hands. Her hair was trimmed and washed and dried. Then Pearl took her over to the

Fitting Room. Ms Martha followed her there. Kaddy was measured and pinned into different models of sleeves and collars. Ms Pearl made her notes. "Okay Martha, you know this is just the preliminary," the bright red lips were saying. "She will have to come back to try on in three days and then I will come up to the House on the Big Day and get her ready myself." Kaddy felt it was too much. "You don't have to dress me. I can do that", she quickly said. "Hush Child!" It was an order from Ms Pearl and there was a hush in the entire shop as she flicked the little fan in her hand. "When you come to Pearl, we get the job done." "Now what time is this Ha Ha Martha?" "Ten in the morning this Sunday", Martha said quietly. "Very well. Very Well", the fan continued to flutter. "We will be there at seven. Now that's settled." "Toni dear have you cleaned up Ms Row yet?" and Ms Pearl moved on to inspect Grandma Maisey in her chair.

"Nice! Nice! Ms Pearl was heard saying. Grandma Maisey looked twenty years younger. Toni had cut her hair to her neck and colored it reddish gold. Grandma's toes and fingers were also done and painted in baby pink tones. Her face was amazing. Everything was different. Her eyebrows were waxed and shaped and so were the hairs under her chin. The dark circles under her eyes were hidden and she had on the perfect foundation that hid the fact that she was made up. She looked fresh and beautiful. Highlighted eyes and bronze pink lips, Grandma Maisey Row now looked like the Mistress of her Mansion. But to Ms Pearl, the job was not complete. "Come with me Maisey", she said and Grandma followed her into the Fitting Room. While Martha and Kaddy waited, Ms Row was measured and fitted and subjected to a session of try ons. She finally emerged wearing comfortable four inch high black shoes, a baby pink two piece skirt suit, a matching black leather clutch and smelling so Avon Gold. "Wow Wee!" Martha said when she saw her. Ms Row smiled. Toni totally approved and hi fived Ms Pearl. The girls put six other outfits into the car and Ms Pearl bid them "Tah tah".

CHAPTER FIFTEEN

Lizze at the Mansion

The rest of the week was hectic. Tents were set up. Gazebos dressed. Chairs decorated. Gardens cleaned. Lots and lots of food preprepared. The mansion was Alive. The 'Lucky' lawyer had arrived and he was introduced around. Lizzie was overwhelmed. She liked the fanfare of the occasion but the realization that she was going to leave mummy and daddy and go to a whole new country with a whole new companion and a whole new house and a whole new life, seemed to daunt her for a while. She came asking for Kaddy on Saturday. Grandma let her into the living room and looked at Kaddy with raised questioning eyebrows. Kaddy hugged Lizzie and asked how she was. They were like old classmates reunited. Kaddy smiled to herself. She could feel the apprehension and nervousness of the poor girl. Kaddy hugged her tightly with all the love she had imagined over the years, loving her as a cousin, as a sister, as a friend. "Why don't you girls take a walk in the gardens", Grandma suggested and they left together. They talked about the wedding and Lizzie talked about Handsome Harold and the gifts he brought her and how he held her hand and how they kissed. They talked and laughed as girls that age should and then Lizzie got quiet and she looked down at her hands in her lap as they sat on a garden bench. "What is wrong?" Kaddy asked. "I am scared Kaddy", Elizabeth confessed. "I am going away all alone. What will happen if babies come? How will I manage?"

"I am so scared", she said again and turned to hug Kaddy's neck and cry on her shoulder. Kaddy was so surprised she wanted to laugh. She patted the crying 'Bride to be' and let her wet her shoulders for a while. "Don't cry Lizzie." Kaddy was trying to console her cousin. "You will not be alone!" "Harold loves you. You are a team now." "Its Harold and Lizzie not Lizzie alone." Kaddy tried to find the right things to say to comfort Miss Elizabeth. "You will be in charge of your own home, fixing it up, cooking nice dishes, being the Hostess to family and friends." The sobbing stopped and Lizzie listened, so Kaddy continued. "And when babies come, Harold would be so excited, he would pamper you and help you and mummy and daddy will visit." Elizabeth straightened her posture, "So its going to be alright?" she asked Kaddy. Kaddy thought for a second and then she turned to the tear streaked cheeks next to her. "My mama's blood group was B positive," she said. Whenever Mama got sick she would tell me, 'Be positive'." That made Lizzie laugh. "That is funny!" she said. "But it is true", Kaddy told her. "You know Harold loves you and you love him too, don't you?" Elizabeth's cheeks reddened and she shyly smiled. "He makes me feel warm inside when he holds my hand and when he looks at me I forget that there are other people around and he tells me I am beautiful." It was Kaddy turn to laugh. "There! You see! You have answered yourself," she said. "You do love him so there is nothing to worry about." "You get dressed up tomorrow and look beautiful and leave the rest to the caterers." Lizzie cleaned up her face and looked bravely ahead. "I guess you are right. Its time for a change in life. I cant be with mummy and daddy always." Then Elizabeth said very quietly in the open air, "Kaddy, I am sorry for being mean when we were younger. Mummy didn't mean the harsh things she said. I am glad you are my cousin. I am so glad you are here." Kaddy stepped off the bench and walked to a nearby rose bush. She snapped off a pretty pink bloom and smelled is fragrant perfume. Lizzie had also gotten up and they walked back to the main house. "I don't regret any of the past Lizzie", Kaddy told her. "I love you and Uncle and Aunt Molly. I am thankful for my time in the Big Shop. The Past is Past and we will not talk about it anymore." They were interrupted by loud voices calling, "Lizzie! Lizzie!" It was Aunt Molly. She caught up with them. She kissed

Lizzie's cheeks and said "Hi Kaddy", to Kaddy. "Lizzie where have you been? We have to fit your dress again and set your veil and aunt Bee is here to do your hair," and with that Aunt Molly pulled Lizzie's arm along. "Bye Kaddy", Molly called over her shoulder. "Bye Kaddy," Lizzie waved and they were gone. All in a day's work Kaddy thought.

CHAPTER SIXTEEN

Getting Dressed Up

Sunday morning arrived with extra special light. "Oh no!" Martha said shaking her head as she looked at the sky. "Could be hot today and rain tonight." Ms Pearl got Kaddy up early. Her hair was to be washed and rolled in a special way. Her face needed the lightest tones of highlight. Kaddy loved her dress. It was pale patterned lilac chiffon over plain lilac silk, with the cutest flyaway sleeves, a mandarin collar and lilac buttons all the way down. There was a matching silk scarf which Ms Pearl tried to fit around Kaddy's twenty inch waist. The dress was close fitted under the bust line and then skirted out into double flairs. The silk felt breezy and free around Kaddy's legs.

Ms Pearl accented the lilac floral with silver and quartz jewelry. Long two inch silver chain earrings with lilac quartz inset and a one inch wide silver band with matching insets for her left hand made the ensemble royal and rich. The outfit was completed with almost flat lighter lilac shoes and a small hand held matching purse. Her hair was a natural reddish brown but when it was done it was this mass of golden reddish curls reaching across her head and down to the middle of her back. On one side behind her ears, Ms Pearl secured the springy curls with a clip of a quartz rose. Lip gloss was added to her lips. Kaddy was truly 'dressed up.' Ms Pearl sprayed her with seductive sultry Avon Soft Musk and she was ready. She looked and felt like a Princess. At 9.00am, Ms Pearl held her arm and walked her to Grandma Maisey's room. She was presented. Grandma was speechless. "Kaddy, you look beautiful!" Maisey finally said. Kaddy smiled. "Thank You! Thank You!" Ms Pearl said as she took a bow. They all laughed. But Kaddy was more struck at the transformation of her grandmother. "Grandma! Look at You!" Kaddy said as she walked around the smugly smiling sixty year old. Maisey was wearing a long burgundy gown. It was not chiffon nor velvet but it moved and it was soft. Ruby and gold earrings made like flowers lay close to her ear lobes. Her hair was light and fluffy. Her eyes were smiling and her cheeks radiant. "I am ready," Maisey said as she stood regal in her velvet burgundy two inch heeled shoes.

"Not quite so ready," a voice said at the door and in walked a dashing gentleman in a dark burgundy pants and suit with a cream shirt. Doc Row was clean shaven and well trimmed. A gold watch was on his wrist and a gold wedding band on the appropriate finger. Kaddy forgot her own embellishments and giggled like a school girl. Harry Row and Maisey Row made the day brighter. "Not quite so ready yet, Maisey love", the Doc said. In his hand was a ruby and gold necklace made with a chain of the same flowers Grandma wore in her ears. As he pinned it around Maisey's open neck, she could only ask repeatedly, "Harry! How could you! How did you? When?" The questions needed no answers. "And one more thing Misses Row," he continued. Kaddy and Ms Pearl looked on. Grandpa Harry reached into his shirt pocket and took out a gold wedding band and showed it to Maisey. "I saved this for you," he said to her and he slipped it unto her finger. Grandma hugged him and she was going to cry. "None of that now," he told her lovingly and he reached down and kissed her ears. Then he turned to Kaddy, "Look at my Granddaughter!" "Where were you hiding?" "Maisey, do you see this beauty?" he asked Grandma. Maisey hugged Kaddy as much as is permitted when people get dressed up. "She looks so much like Haley," Grandma said. "No crying now woman," Doc said again gently. "It is a happy day. Let us go join the others."

The Mansion was alive. People were on all the chairs and gardens. Ribbons and flowers and balloons waved in the breeze. Kaddy was not the kind of child accustomed to being dressed and put to sit in a crowd. She made her way to Martha's kitchen. Martha was brand new with earrings and bracelets and stockings and a new fancy red wig. Kaddy teased her. Martha had seen the beauty in Kaddy from the first time she saw her. What was most alluring was that the child was not aware of her good looks and her shyness and modesty were like honey on a lemon cake. "You look quite spiffy yourself'" Martha told Kaddy as she sat in her lilac loveliness at the table in the kitchen. "So what are you doing in my kitchen?" the housekeeper asked. Kaddy sat and played with the bracelet on her wrist. "Do you think he will come?" she asked Martha. "If you are not out there how will you ever know," Martha said and she playfully pushed Kaddy out of the kitchen and unto the bustling grounds. Kaddy did not for a second forget that she could see Andy Pero again very soon. She met Uncle Raymond as she walked to the assembled chairs. He looked well in his suit and nosegay. "Kaddy! Is that you!" he said as she hugged him and then he hurried away. Kaddy took a seat at the back. Young men were starting to look her way. Ben, the video camera guy whistled in half tone. They had met earlier in the week. "Look at you Sweet Kaddy!" and he aimed his camera full into her face. She made to shoo him with her purse and he laughed and left to take pictures at the front of the assembly. A small band played music to get the guests settled. Drinks and appetizers were served to those who needed. Kaddy watched as a group of children played hop scotch on the soft grass.

Martha dusted and washed her hands. That was the last puff pastry in the oven. Most of the work was done by hired help but she had to see that people did what they had to do. It was a quarter to ten. She took off her apron and decided to walk around. She knew many of the people in the gathering. Many Hi's and hellos, many cheeks to kiss and hands to shake. Martha got to the decorated gate and looked up and down the road. Cars were still arriving. She turned to go back to the kitchen and took a path through the back gardens.

CHAPTER SEVENTEEN

Finding a Princess

In a small gazebo partly hidden from the view of the assembly, there was a young man sitting with his head bent over his open legs as he looked at some paper he held with both hands in his lap. He had taken off his light grey suit jacket and his white shirt was unbuttoned four buttons down. It was probably the program for the ceremony. Young men usually did not like to wait around in assemblies.

"Hi there!" Martha called out. "Not going to join the others, Its almost time." The young man laughed and got to his feet. "Hi there yourself!" he said as he walked down the three steps to Martha. Thick black hair, twinkling black eyes, hair on the chest, charming mischievous smile. He is a really nice lad, Martha thought.

"Why are you hiding here?" she asked. He slung the grey jacket across his shoulder and stopped in front of Martha. "It has been a long journey. I am tired and hot." "Can I bother you for something cold to drink" he asked. "Sure!" Martha smiled, "If you don't mind having it in a kitchen." "What! Its my favourite part of the house," he said as he fell into step and they walked together to the kitchen. Martha got a pitcher of lemon iced tea all ready from the fridge. She put it on a tray with a tall glass. She seated the young lad at the small table in the kitchen and took the tray to him. "Something smells really good", he told her. "My God!" she said as she turned to the oven. She had forgotten the pastry shells. They were dark golden brown but not burnt. They would have extra crispiness but they were not ruined. After she had saved the pastry and put them away she put together a tray of sandwiches and cakes and took it to the kitchen table. The young man was looking at the paper again. Matha put the tray down and asked him. "May I join you?" "Sure! I welcome it", he said as he moved to pull out the other chair facing him for Ms Martha. Charming and well mannered, Martha thought. "What do you have there?" she asked pointing to the paper in his hand. He hesitated and then he passed the paper to her. "Can you help me find this Princess?" he said with a short laugh.

Sixty three year old Martha felt a flush right through her as she looked down at the colored sketch of a young woman wearing a pale peach dress. The reddish brown hair and the medium brown eyes were so familiar to Martha. "Who is she?" Martha asked. The young man laughed. He looked into the kind old eyes in front of him and he wanted to tell her. He wanted to talk about the girl he had met for two minutes, a girl sweet and fragile, with resilient eyes, a girl who filled his dreams with visions of her peach dress. He told a story Martha had heard before. Now she heard his love and his pain and his yearning.

When he was almost through, Martha asked, "So what do you do for a living?" "I am an artist," the young man said with pride. Martha did not know whether to laugh out loud or scream. "What!" she said in a too loud voice. The young man defended his position. "Well, my paying job is Engineering. I manage my Dad's firm in the Capital. Building Engineering," he explained, "But I love to paint", he added as he leaned back in his chair. Martha shook her head as she still looked at the paper he had given to her. "So what will you do if you find your Princess," Martha asked as she gave him back his sketch . . . . And in walked Kaddy. "Martha! I saw you greeting the crowd. I cant stay out there any longer," and Kaddy slipped off her shoes and stood up and looked straight at . . . Him. He just stared at her. "It is You!" he said. He turned to Ms Martha. "Its Her!"

He looked at Kaddy and then waved his sketch to her. "It is You!" Kaddy stood in all her fresh aired beauty, rooted to the spot. It was Him! He was sitting in her kitchen! He looked sooo sweet. What was she to say? He stood up and reached her and held her by the arms as he looked at her. "You are Kaddy?" he asked gently. "She shook her head in agreement and blushed. "I have tried to find you", he was saying in that same warm voice. "Something happened that night," he said in almost a a whisper. "Did you feel any thing?" he asked in the same whisper. Kaddy backed away. She looked at a speechless Martha. No help there! He followed her in the spacious kitchen. "Please tell me how you feel," he said to her as he stood close without touching her. "I think I love you so much", she heard him say in From the Heart seriousness. Kaddy found herself with her back against the tall refrigerator. She needed to open it and hide behind the cold melons and grapes. He stood close in front of her. She looked at him, deep into those black eyes. She loved him. She knew nothing about him but she loved him and he was standing there saying he loved her. He held her shoulders with both hands on either side and brought his lips to touch hers. She resisted for a moment. He kissed just her lips gently as if asking her permission and her arms reached up around his neck as she moved closer and let him kiss his doubts away. It was better than all imagination. It was like the sweetest sharing. He hugged her to his chest and put his face in her sweet smelling curls. "I love you so much", he said again and again. And then Miss Martha called his name. "Andy!" "Andy!!" she said louder. He freed his head but not his arms as he turned to look at Miss Martha. She approached them and put a hand up to his querulous expression. "Yes I know who you are Andy Pero", she said. "You two come here", and she guided them to the small dining table and made them sit in separate chairs. "Now you two moving too fast here, you need to know more about each other," she said and Delia ran into the kitchen and whispered into Ms Martha's ears. Martha looked angry and impatient. "What is wrong?" Kaddy asked. "Its nothing Miss Kaddy," Delia said, "its only my Mama. She drank too much punch and she took over Pastor's Station and we cant have the wedding yet." "Please don't be angry with Mama Miss Kaddy please", Delia pleaded, "she means no harm. She just loves a big wedding." Martha was putting on her apron in a hurry. "That Silvie!" she muttered, "warned her to stay away from the punch." "Stop chattering Delia! Martha said harshly. "You go on now. I am coming", and Martha shooed Delia out of the door.

Martha then turned to Andy and Kaddy. "You two behave!" She said as she pointed her fingers at them. "I am coming back to deal with this."

It took Martha and four large gentlemen fifteen minutes to get a singing Silvie into a car and away to her home. No one complained. It was good entertainment and the bride had not yet appeared. Poor Harold had taken a seat next to Uncle Raymond at the front of the assembly.

Fifteen minutes was a long time for Andy Stephen Pero and Maryam Kaddy Wills. Kaddy had taken Andy up to the room her mom and dad had lived in. It was easier to explain her life by showing it to him. He had kissed her many more times and he kept looking at her and telling her how beautiful she was. "Will you marry me Miriam Kaddy?" he asked again and again. She did not answer him but they moved to the window overlooking the gardens and looked out. And then she heard them calling her name on the public address system. It was Uncle Raymond's voice. "Kaddy! Kaddy! Where are you child? Lizzie is calling for you." "Oh Dear!" Kaddy said as she turned to Andy, "I have to go." "Lizzie must be having cold feet again", and before he could say anything, she kissed his lips and hurried down the stairs. She met Ms Martha coming half way up and Martha gave her a mean look. "We were good", Kaddy said with a teasing smile and ran all the way down.

CHAPTER EIGHTEEN

A Wedding Delayed

It was late and the crowd was restless. They had been humored with Silvie's booze bout and now they wanted to know who Kaddy was and why she was needed by the Bride. Kaddy emerged from the front porch and almost ran down the length of the assembly to a waiting Uncle Raymond. Ben swung his camera to catch her run and as he whistled playfully, the entire assembly got to whistling and clapping. Uncle Raymond took her to the room behind the Pastor's station. Lizzie and Aunt Molly were hugging each other and crying. As Lizzie entered, they turned to look her way. Her dressed up appearance seemed to shock them for a while. Then Elizabeth rushed to her and hugged her tightly. "Kaddy, I don't know how to do it!" Lizzie wailed. "I don't know how to leave Mummy and Daddy." Aunt Molly had cold feet as well. "I don't know how I will live without her", she was saying. Kaddy pulled Lizzie to the heavy curtains that hid the room from the rest of the assembly. "Look out there Liz! Look At Harold." She told Lizzie. "He has been waiting, waiting to see you walk to him. Look at your Papa. He wants to see you settled well." Elizabeth looked out and then back to her crying mother. In her mind she had to choose between her parents and a stranger. Kaddy realized the dilemma of the Bride's logic. Kaddy opened the curtains and called to uncle Raymond to get Grandma Maisey. The problem was aunt Molly. Someone older had to make her see sense.

Grandma came and tried her best. It was already 11.00am. They were an hour late.

CHAPTER NINETEEN

Two Weddings at the Mansion

Elizabeth had decided to take the easy road of putting off all the white silk and muslin and going home with Mommy. As Grandma and Kaddy wondered what to do next, voices were heard asking for permission to enter. It was Andy Pero and Grandpa Harry. The small dressing room was suddenly crowded. Aunt Molly got to her feet and tried to smooth out her designer Mother of the Bride skirt suit. Uncle Raymond was concerned about his wife's blood pressure. He had asked Doc to check on her. Doc Harry with his Doctor's bag in hand hugged Aunt Molly. "Come Moll", he said with expert gentleness, as he took her to another chair in the room. Her BP was elevated. He called for some water and gave her tablets right away to get it down and stabilized. That upset Elizabeth even more. She started crying again blaming herself for causing her mother's BP to go up. Doc knew that crying was no good for Molly so he tried to calm Lizzie. She clung to her mother and they held on to each other. Doc looked over to Grandma Maisey and shook his head. He didn't know what more to do. Kaddy was quiet since Andy came into the room. Her own heart was racing. He searched for her eyes the moment he entered and she could feel him watching her.

She was shy and uncomfortable. All her relatives were there. How could she explain him to them. He had managed to move next to her and hold her hand. She pulled away afraid that they would be seen but he held on as she hid her hand behind her back. He bent his head to her ear and told her he loved her. Then Andy Pero went to Doc Harry and they spoke briefly very quietly. Then Andy went to Aunt Molly and shook her hand. She remembered him. Andy then raised his hand in greeting to Elizabeth and he spoke to her.

'Lizzie, you look very beautiful today in your dress and Harold has been waiting to see you." He then paused and lowered his voice while still making it very clear.

"Will it be easier to go get married if Kaddy got married too?" There was a unison of "What!" from Grandma and Kaddy.

Elizabeth smiled. The idea appealed to her. If she was going to the 'gallows', nice to take someone with her . . . . She was not going to make a mistake alone. Any other girl might have been upset to share her wedding day but Elizabeth And Aunt Molly had a different mental processing system. Suddenly the tears were gone. Now Lizzie was in a hurry. Andy Pero walked over to a confused Kaddy. He got down on one knee and held her hand. "Miriam Kaddy Wills will you please marry me?" he asked. Kaddy watched him on his knees and was more bewildered. She was afraid to look up. Grandma and Grandpa were there. Uncle Raymond and Aunt Molly and Elizabeth were there. All her family must be equally confused but no questions were asked. Andy was still on his knees. Then Grandma came over to Kaddy and said in her ear.

"We all know baby. Andy has spoken to us and he asked our permission and your Uncle's too. He loves you very much."

Kaddy looked at the Kneeling Pero and she too kneeled on the hard floor of the Pastor's Station. He held both of her hands in his and spoke quietly. "Please Kaddy, I don't want to lose any more time without you. I love you. Please say yes." Kaddy looked into his eyes and saw true love there. She leaned forward and kissed him and told him for the first time she loved him. He was ecstatic with joy and held her to him and stood up and spun her around. "So you will marry Me?" he asked again. "Yes I will", she said and held on to him. Then Aunt Molly stopped them. "You two wait one minute now!" All eyes waited. She searched through her handbag and produced a silver wedding band from a giftbox. She gave it to Andy. "Its brand new from Avon", she said and everyone laughed. The men then left the room and in came Ms Pearl and Martha. Ms Pearl had come prepared with extra dresses and accessories for any wedding emergency. She had a white Chinese silk coat studded with beadwork and rhinestones. Added to the lilac dress, the outfit looked bridal. Martha pinned a short veil to a thirty five year old tiara. It was Grandma Maisey's. Aunt Molly stepped out to the garden and arranged a pink rose bud and babe's breath and green fern bouquet. Pearl added matching lilac ribbons.

Grandma helped Elizabeth get her long trail back in place and powder her face again. She gave her the yellow roses and green ribboned bouquet already prepared and the Brides were ready. It was 11.30am. Uncle Raymond came in and kissed both girls. "You sure about this?" he asked Kaddy. She shook her head. "Okay! Lets get things done! he said and left. The voice on the P.A system was making the announcement. There would be two weddings. The crowd got to its feet with slow clapping. Pastor stood with his robes and Holy Book. Harold and Andy took their places on either side of him. The heavy curtains parted and the clapping grew louder. It was Grandpa Harry with Aunt Molly and Grandma Maisey on either arm. He took them to their seats at the front of the assembly. He then joined Uncle Raymond behind the curtains. "This is it girls!" Grandpa said. Elizabeth was ready. Uncle Raymond took her arm and kissed her forehead. Grandpa hugged Kaddy and hooked his arm in hers. The Band played "Here comes the Bride" and the guest clapped their palms out. Raymond went out first and gave Elizabeth to Harold. Then Grandpa walked out with Kaddy and took her to Andy Pero. He held her hands tightly in his as they stood beside Pastor and waited. The music stopped and Pastor raised his hand to the crowd for silence.

"Its time now, for some serious Holy business", he said. In five minutes, Lizzie became Mrs Elizabeth Mire wife of Mr Harold Charles Mire. Pastor then turned to Andy Stephen Pero. When he slipped the Avon Silver band on her finger, Kaddy felt complete, accomplished. There was so much love in his eyes and his touch, Kaddy felt shy. In another five minutes she became Mrs Andy Stephen Pero.

CHAPTER TWENTY

New Beginnings

The guests ate and danced and ate and danced. Lizzie was happy. She had forgotten her tears. She kept looking at the expensive white gold and diamond rings, Harold had placed on her finger. She was married. She had a husband who was a good lawyer. Her parents loved him and he loved her. She felt she had done very well.

Uncle Raymond hugged Aunt Molly to him as they danced slowly. He and Moll had gone through hard times. He was already thinking to sell the Big Shop and go live in the Big Country. He knew Moll. She would hurt to be far from Lizzie. She had made that child her world. He wanted them to get away from the shop and find love again. He kissed her head as they waltzed through the next number.

Grandpa and Grandma Row were two stepping slowly on the dance floor. It was a long day but things went well. Maisey put her head on Harry's shoulder. "I love you Harry Row", she said as they danced. "Keep saying it Maisey Row", Doc laughed, "I love you too Pet." "Do you know that Andy is an artist too?" Grandma told him. "We did it right this time", Doc said.

Miriam Kaddy took her Andy to the garden at the back to meet mama and papa. She stared at the headstones that said, "Here lies Haley Wills", "Here lies Andrew Wills." The girl who had been counseling and putting things right for everyone started to cry. "Oh Maman! Oh Maman!" she kept saying as she fell to her knees in the garden. There was an ache in her stomach. She missed her mama. Kaddy stood up and leaned on the white picket fence around the graves.

Andy held her close. He was crying too. He felt her loss, he felt her pain. He wanted to give her so much love to make her forget her past. He wanted to see her running around with laughing children at her heels. He scattered the petals of the rose buds of her bouquet that Kaddy brought to give her parents. He spoke to them He told them he loved Kaddy very much and he wanted to take care of her. Through her tears Kaddy said, "Maman, I love him very much." A soft petal that lay on the earth flew upward and touched Kaddy's cheek. Andy put out his arm and caught it before it flew off again and he looked at Miriam Kaddy Pero. "That was Mama," she said smiling, "she approves." "I know." Andy whispered at her head. He kissed the petal and placed it back on the earthy bed. "Thank You", he said quietly as he closed the garden gate.

Miriam Kaddy put her hand in his as they walked away. She looked up to the sky and the gathering clouds. "Thank You!" she said with all the voices in her. "Thank You My God, for everything."

THE END

THE GOD FACTOR

The greatest love…. stories you may consider yet to be written,
Yet unaware are we of the Greatest love in our midst, the love of one who
knows the full meaning of love and who alone can teach us the meaning
of true Love.

The Master of our Creation lovingly moulds everyone of us
Then puts us in the free air and expansive earth
And watches us grow.
He gives, He forgives, He loves.

And He tests.
How can there be love without trial and reward!
How can there be enjoyment and understanding without
pain and sacrifice!

And yet He stands by us in all of it.
He shows us the way through it all.
He, Power of the Universe, asks,
What does my servant want from me?
Only the Greatest love can do this.

He is Supreme, Merciful and Kind, Allah is.
His love is always knowing and just and aware.
We bow in humility and warmth and imploding emotion.
What love is this but the Greatest ever.

What love is this that fills my heart and overflows my tears.
What love is this that sent men like me to show me the way.
This is but the Greatest.

Wild with passion I submit,
Crying out His name to all. Ya Allah!
In Mercy you created us that we may serve a term appointed,
And then to the Supreme triumph,
Resplendent in fine raiment along banks of scented musk,
A reward in Jannah forever.
What love is this but the Greatest.

On Earth you join our hearts that we may find also comfort and passion,
And laughter and happiness in mates of our kind.
In your Selfless Greatness you allow us to love each other,
While fulfilling your ordinance and still loving you.
What love is this but the Greatest.

Only the Greatest one can give us good here and good in the hereafter.
Only the Greatest can keep love true and sweet and unwavering.
Only He sees the anguish and hears the cry of the sad heart that longs
for the absent love.
And only He can bring them back together in his Perfect Plan.
This is the Greatest love.

Years fade to minutes as lovers unite.
A kiss, an embrace…ways of us mortals,
And He is all Aware.

He shows us the way to each other,
So we can be thankful and love Him more.

Oh Allah! Most Beautiful, Most Loving,
Help us to accept the ways of your love,
And bless us in the love you give us for our companions.
Teach us to love you more,
And guide us to all that is good and true.
Oh My Allah, yours is the Greatest Love.
Ameen.

NAJ

CHAPTER ONE

Ramadhan

"Allah o Akbar"! Zaman raised his hands in Qiyam to start his Asr salaat. It was already 5.15pm. The calendar said Sunset would be early at 5.55pm. It was Ramadhan. Zaman was observing his fast and he had fallen asleep in the hot afternoon. This was not his usual routine, he should have been doing some Zikr but he was tired and worried. His fourteen year old daughter Salma had left to go visit with her cousins since 9.00am that morning. She had promised to be good and return early to prepare the dinner for the breaking of the fast. Zaman was not really concerned with dinner even though it had been a hard day and he was hungry. He usually went to the Masjid to break the fast with the other people of the Village. Very tasty food was cooked every day at the Masjid to feed the fasting. Zaman was worried about Salma. She was his only child and taking care of her was not easy. Her mother left the home when she was a puny four year old. Now she was a tall beauty of fourteen. Just as he was saying his Ameen to end his Duaa, he heard car doors open and close. He got up and peeped through the curtains at the window. It was Salma and "that boy" again. Zaman felt the energy leave his body. He felt defeated and exhausted. Why didn't his beautiful child listen to him? He talked to her. He explained and she promised, "Yes Daddy, I would be good." Now it was Ramadhan. He knew his nosy neighbors were looking out and listening.

"Ya Allah!" he sighed. He could not run away from this. Her mother had done that. Naj had just left him with a four year old. She just left. He had been so hurt and angry, he never dwelled much on the happenings of that day. He carried on. He worked and washed and cooked and cleaned. He helped with homework and examinations and PTA meetings. His sister Asma was busy with six young children and expecting a seventh. He had two brothers, Abu and Zaheer who had migrated to the USA. Salma had left to go help Asma. Now here she was coming home with this boy, in his car, to the front gate. Zaman repeated "Allahu Akbar", and tried to calm himself. He heard Salma close the door and go to the kitchen. Then he heard her footsteps as she climbed the stairs to the upper flat where he was. He moved to the top of the stairs and looked down. The pretty black eyes looked up at him. "Assalamualaikum Daddy, I was looking for you." She stopped halfway up aware of his anger. He pointed a finger at her and kept shaking it. "No Dad! Its not what you think! He saw me on the road and he gave me a lift. Honest Dad! Call Aunt Asma. I just left there and she sent dinner." Playful black eyes looked straight at him and Zaman knew she spoke the truth. He felt the pressure in his head ease. He started down the steps and past the child to get into the kitchen. Salma followed him. Zaman sat at the small table in the kitchen. He looked at the two bags Salma had placed there.

"Please don't be angry Dad," she was saying, "I wanted to get home early. Zaid is fasting too. He was on his way to the Masjid and he saw me waiting for a bus. He had his father in the car with him. I promised you Dad. I didn't do anything wrong." Salma went to her father and hugged him. He had not said anything and she could not take it when he was not talking to her. Zaman loved this child so much. He hugged her back and then she pulled away. She playfully pointed a finger waving it to him, "You did not answer my Salam." she told him. Zaman laughed and said, "Walaikumassalam! What did your Aunt make? Salma opened the bags. She glanced at the kitchen clock. It was 5.50pm. She liked when her dad was at home to break the fast. "I will set up the dastakan", she told Zaman. He helped her lay out the small leather sheet on the floor of a part of the kitchen reserved for eating. She put the hot curried chicken and warm soft roti that she had helped Aunty Asma to make, into two separate dishes and placed them on the dastakan. Zaman put some dates and a jug of water in a tray and put that down as well. Salma turned on the stove so she could reheat the tea in the kettle. Five minutes to spare before she could eat and break the fast. Salma loved Ramadhan. Some days she did feel very hungry but it was great to sit at evening and drink that hot tea and know that she did it. She loved the Eid at the end of Ramadhan. It was exciting to check for the new moon to see whether there was more fasting or feasting and gifts. But there was always a sadness too. She had begun to feel that last year when she awoke on the second of Shaawal, the day after the Eid and realized there was no more special Ramadhan fasting. There was always Sunnah fasts every Monday and Thursday and the six days of Shaawal and other special times throughout the year, but Ramadhan fasting was very special. This was Salma's fourth year of fasting. Her memories were all with her dad. He was a good dad and she felt safe with him. She was happy when he was happy. The clock said 5.53pm. They sat on either side of the laid out meal on the floor. Salma poured out two small glasses of water and two cups of hot sweetened tea. Dad had explained the importance of making proper Duaas at the time of Iftar and as they waited she did her silent Zikr, praising Almighty Allah for another day of fasting almost at an end. Zaman watched the small hands as she put things in order. He and his little Salma. He closed his eyes and made his zikr, continuously repeating praises to Allah. Then the clock alarmed. It was set to do that at the time for Iftar. Salma smiled, said Alhamdulilah and they each said their duaa. Zaman took a large date, peeled off half of its brown juicy flesh and saying Bismillah, put it into his mouth. He then drank some water in three sips.

Salma loved dates. It was the one thing she asked her Uncles Abu and Zaheer to send for her from New York, big Majool dates. She and dad would break the fast with dates and water. Then they would pray the Magrib salaat, eat dinner and then go to the Masjid for the Esha and Taraweeh salaat. The Masjid in the village was full for Ramadhan. There was a section for Muslim men and a separate section for Muslim woman. Through a public address system the worshippers followed the Imam as he lead the prayers. The Taraweeh salaat was done in twenty rakaats only in Ramadhan. Sometimes it would take a long time as most Masjids tried to complete the reading of the whole Quran in the Taraweeh prayers of

Ramadhan. Most nights the prayers ended between 9.00-10.00pm and Salma would go home with her dad. They were usually so tired they fell asleep soon after they got home. But tonight Zaman was restless. It was almost 12.00 midnight and he could not sleep. Salma was tired after helping her aunt that she fell asleep on the way home. He had to fetch her up the stairs and put her in her bed. He could hear her snoring. He teased her about that and promised to record her. She didn't like to be told that she snored in her sleep.

CHAPTER TWO

Remembering Naj

Zaman was worried. He and Naj were married when she was eighteen and he was twenty five. In one year they had Salma. Naj left when she was four. Now she was fourteen. Zaman was going on forty. He never had the time or interest to court another woman. Naj made him distrust all women. How could he start over with a strange person? Who would love his Salma and treat her well? He could not take chances with his child. Salma was growing up. She was very pretty. He did not like the friendship she had with Zaid Abdullah. Zaman did not want her thinking about boys or being near one. So much could go wrong. He remembered the night Salma was born. Naj had bad pains all day. The Village Midwife checked with her and finally decided that they had to get to a hospital to do a C section. So quickly everything happened. Naj was wheeled into the operating room and in five minutes they pulled the bloody bundle out. He heard the little cry and they gave her to him. Naj had Blood pressure and Blood sugar problems and she had to remain in the hospital for extra days. Zaman stayed at the hospital looking after the tiny newborn for three days and nights while Naj got better.

Zaman shook his head back to the present. He did not want to remember the past but the past would not leave his head. He never thought about Naj. In all the ten years he let himself be angry and let anger justify his actions. For ten years he had locked away memories, now a door had opened and he could see the Smile of Naj, he could smell the Perfume of Naj, he could feel the Hands of Naj . . . . He had no tears in ten years, now Zaman put his face in his pillow and cried like a wounded puppy.

In that first year his Naj was every dream fulfilled, every desire satisfied. She would cook and feed it to him, she would soothe his whole body massaging with those little hands she had and she made him want her over and over. He could feel her love in her eyes and her kisses and her touch. It excited him to see a woman love him so much. He wasn't surprised when she said she was going to have a baby after only two months of marriage. She was the sexiest, most attractive woman with that child growing inside of her. Sometimes he could feel his heart pounding in his chest just looking at her.

But things changed. It was after the sixth month of the pregnancy, Naj changed. She got bigger and bigger. She was always angry. His 98 pound wife was weighing over 200 pounds. She did not want to work with him or even be with him in the grocery store they owned. Every day she would cry and ask for something new. She needed new clothes and a new big bed and new furniture and he had to build a separate apartment downstairs for her. Doctors and friends told him it was hormone changes of the pregnancy but those days were terrible and they did not stop when Salma was born. Naj did not breast feed her own baby.

Zaman felt the tension and stress come back to him. It was ugly living the next four years. He had to hire people to clean and cook while he worked in the shop. Somehow Salma was kept alive. Naj would feed her and keep her clean and watch over her but he wondered sometimes if a mother could dislike her own child.

He and Naj just existed. His desire and love were turned off with the fatty appearance. She had this flabby bulging tummy and her arms were saggy and her face and neck were all fat. Zaman hated himself for the way he felt but he could not help it.

He sat up in his bed and remembered. He had not spoken to her in two weeks although she slept in the same bed with him. She came to him one night and tried to do everything she knew he liked. She asked him to forgive her. She told him she loved him. He closed his eyes and listened to her voice. Even that had changed to a hoarseness. He needed a woman that night and he fulfilled his needs. He fell asleep for a while and when he awoke he could hear her crying quietly. In the morning she was gone. There was not a letter, not a note, not a call. He didn't call her family either. He had a four year old pulling at his pants for breakfast and potty and school. Life had to go on and it did. Zaman felt remorse and guilt and numbness. Ten years seemed like a week ago. In his mind he never could divorce Naj. She was Salma's mother. He did not want to make a decision about that part of his life. Somehow it would be fixed. It was crazy living with an absent wife. Where did she go? What did she do? What did she want him to do? Eventually he closed the grocery store and became a farmer. He had acres of land from his parents and he planted peppers and shallots and lettuce and long beans and even some pine apples. There were large trees laden with different fruit at different times. It was very hard work but it paid well sometimes and it was what he needed to let life go on.

Zaman got up and checked the clock. It was 1.30am in the morning of a new day. He took a cold shower and went to his prayer rug. Allah was the Forgiver and the Guide. Zaman needed to talk to his Lord. He spent more than an hour praying and begging and crying to Allah for Forgiveness and guidance. He prayed for Naj. Wherever she was she was still his wife. A Nikah is a serious bond. He had a wife somewhere. He wondered where.

CHAPTER THREE

Bibi and Mai and Uzaid

Maimoona was Zaman's mother. New York was cold this November but she got up to get food ready for the fast. She and her youngest two sons Abu and Zaheer had migrated to the United States of America fifteen years ago. She had overstayed a visitors visa permit and was therefore an illegal immigrant. If she left the USA she would not be allowed back in. She was 'in hiding', afraid to be found and living a secluded life in New York. She could not call her eldest son Zaman who lived in her home country very often. She used pay phones on the street and paid with a calling card. She could not give an address and have mail delivered to her. At any time she could be stopped by a Police Officer on a New York corner and asked for identification and entry status. She could be jailed in a US prison or sent home as a deportee. Her sons Abu and Zaheer were also 'in hiding' until the last five years.

They struggled to survive working at jobs for below the minimum wage because they had no legal status to work. They lived with Maimoona in a one bedroom basement made for one person. The boys slept on folding cots on the floor and their mother took the small room. She cooked, cleaned, did the laundry and took care of the neighbor's kids. They managed, they saved. Both sons married two American citizen girls and an expensive lawyer was putting their immigration status in order. An Immigration amnesty was announced in the USA as the country prepared for new elections. Maimoona was to become a US citizen after fifteen Winters. All she could dream about was going home to see her son and her granddaughter she never got to hold.

When she got to the kitchen, the fire was already going under the tea kettle. Bibi was up early. "God Bless that child", Maimoona thought. Bibi was the reason the aging grandmother smiled more often these days. Mai as Bibi called her, had high blood pressure problems and she suffered loss of movement in her limbs and had to be taken to a Queen's Hospital in New York. Bibi was a nurse and health care attendant on duty that day. Over a period of months as Mai visited for treatment Bibi got to know most of Mai's story and they realized that they were from the same native country. Mai was unhappy having to live with one of her married sons and his American wife who could not 'understand' Maimoona. Bibi invited the grandmother to move into her three bedroom first floor apartment in which she lived with her son. They were together for almost a year. This was their first Ramadhan. Mai bumped into Uzaid as he was coming from the bathroom. "Assalamualaikum Grandma," he told her. "Walaikumassalam son", Mai said as she squeezed his shoulder. He was a good son to his mother, very mannerly and already keeping whole day fasts. Maimoona did not ask many questions about Uzaid's father and Bibi did not explain. "He is not with us", she said once. Mai did not know if that meant that he was dead or away or divorced. But there were no male visitors or callers to the house all the time she was there. Mai did not ask more questions.

Together they had a good Ramadhan and a beautiful cold Eid. In December Maimoona became a Naturalized US citizen and she was sworn in and given her new Blue passport. She wanted to go home. Bibi decided to go with her. Maimoona was very very happy. They all got tickets to go home in January.

CHAPTER FOUR

New Yorkers come Home

Zaman was also excited. They had come through the Ramadhan and Eid and he and Salma were on their way to the airport to get Mama Maimoona. He felt like a ten year old. He didn't realize how much he missed his mother. Carefully he drove his van and parked close to the gates.

Salma was excited but cautious. She and daddy had lived well together for all the life she could remember. She hoped Grandma would not upset things.

She told herself to stop those thoughts. It was nice to have a grandmother. She never met anyone from her mother's family. Her only memory of her mother was a lullaby she used to sing to put Salma to sleep. Dad said long ago, "Mama has gone away." They did not talk about her. Salma did not ask. Life went on.

Bibi helped Mai down the stairs and out the doors to the tropical sunshine. It was an early morning flight. Coming from the Cold January to the bright sunshine made them start sweating. They collected their documents and moved to the welcoming area. Bibi felt her stomach contract in nervousness. She had not been home in nine years. He hugged her son to her and he looked up questioningly. She stood tall in her traditional Islamic long green gown and matching scarf. She added sunshades for her eyes. The sunshine was very bright and different from that of New York. Bibi inhaled deeply and said a prayer in her heart. She cast a look up to the clear skies. "Guide my step my words, my thoughts and my actions Oh Merciful Creator," she said as they walked out to look for familiar faces. Maimoona was so happy. She was crying and waving her scarf. Zaman and Salma hugged her. Mai was a wreck over Salma. She kept hugging her and looking at her and hugging her again. Bibi felt tears down her own cheeks. Maimoona introduced them. Bibi hugged Salma close. Salma pulled away and watched Uzaid. He had mischief in his face. She instantly did not like him. Bibi never intended going home with them. Mai insisted and insisted and so it was that they all drove to the same house. On the way, Grandma told the story of how she met Bibi and Bibi saw Zaman check her a couple times through the rear view mirror. Bibi was not comfortable. She tried to tell Mai but the happy grandmother would not have it. "The house has six bedrooms", Mai insisted. Bibi realized that she could not leave Mai alone on the first day back so she decided to stay. Zaman also insisted. She guessed it was some good manners and more curiosity on his part.

Uzaid was adventurous and full of energy. He walked with Zaman and asked about everything he saw. This made Salma very angry. Too many people had intruded into her life. Bibi tried to start a conversation with the teenager but Salma left to the security of her closed room.

One day turned into a week and they were still all together in the same house. Bibi blamed her son for her predicament. He wanted to see the farm and all day he would be out with Zaman. Bibi was left to do the cooking and cleaning and washing and taking care of grandma Maimoona. Bibi had to leave. She was able to dwell without much contact with Zaman. He left early and was home very late, but she noticed him watching her many times. She wore her long clothes and covered her head all the while. He was asking questions about where she lived and who her people were. Bibi explained that her people were all in the USA and she had an old aunt who lived in the country. It was all true.

When the weekend came, Bibi was packed and ready to leave. She had to be firm. She told Mai nicely that Zaman and Salma needed time alone with her. They had not seen her for so long. Maimoona agreed. She had been observing Salma. That young girl needed some 'talking to'. Bibi also declined Zaman's invitation to drive her. She called a taxi herself and left with an unwilling Uzaid. He wanted to help Zaman reap tomatoes, but Bibi was firm. It was time to leave.

CHAPTER FIVE

Mother K

Aunty Khairool or Mother K as she was known in the village, was eighty four years old and lived in a remote part of the country. A small three bedroom cottage stood unfenced surrounded by miles and miles of rice and cane and pasture land. Cattle wandered freely in the pasture. It all belonged to Aunty Khairool. She was half asleep in the old hammock swinging under the house when Bibi got there. "Assalamualaikum", Bibi called out as she walked up to the hammock. "Waalaikumassalam", the wrinkled face replied as she raised herself and stood up. Bibi hugged her warmly and then they turned to Uzaid. The old white haired lady pulled him to her spongy tummy and muttered in Urdu through her tears. Uzaid tried to free himself and walked through the yard to the sprawling land. Bibi was worried as he set off but Mother K said, "Let him go. Chico would look after him." Chico was the faithful short hair common breed dog that got up and and followed Uzaid as he set out to the back. The dog barked and Uzaid turned around. His eyes lit up and he rubbed the dog's head and ears. They smiled together and set off to the pastures. Bibi hugged Aunty Khairool and they went inside. "How are you child?" the old lady asked. "That boy grow up so nice. How come you come back here?"

Bibi sat on a wooden stool and watched her aunt poke the coals in the fireside. There was an old saucepan with cow's milk there getting warm. On one hole of the fireside was a pot of old gooey pepperpot.

Old K put some into a deep dish and then reached over her head for thick bread she had wrapped in clean cotton and stored in a straw basket hanging on a hook from the roof. She broke off a good chunk of a loaf and put it with the pepperpot on a tray and gave it to Bibi. She then sat in the hammock up stairs and waited for answers. Bibi put some bread into the gooey stew and scooped up a chewy soft piece of meat and put it into her mouth. Nobody made pepperpot like Aunty K. Its taste could not be described. A person could live on that alone she used to say. In nine years Bibi had not had that taste. Old K watched her and chuckled. "Fat child, I can wait to hear your story." Bibi ate unashamedly until the bowl was clean. She took it to the sink and washed her hands with water from a bucket. Then she added her weight to the small frame in the hammock and they rocked. Bibi told her aunt about all that happened in the past years. She told her about her training as a nurse, about the apartment, about Uzaid and school and she told her about Maimoona and meeting her in New York and coming home with her and staying at the house.

Aunty Khairool shook her head from side to side and laughed in a non laughing way. "Allah! Allah! Allah!" she said over and over. "So why you really here child? Why you come back now? That man still vex with woman," the old hands told her as they stroked Bibi's hair. "And you walked out and left a daughter," the voice continued. "Girl children hard to forgive. That Salma hard to crack. Don't know what to tell you."

Bibi put her head on the old shoulders and hugged the only person who stood by her ten years ago. She had come to this door scorned and scared and Aunty K took her in and mothered her and helped her. Bibi had to hide her fears and feelings and herself from the world for nine years, now she let it go as she cried and cried. She walked out that morning and hid in this house. Three weeks after she realized that she was pregnant. Aunty Khairool attended to her. She made her lose weight even as the baby grew. She made her special teas with herbs that controlled her pressure and sugar problems. Uzaid was delivered in this cottage by those sure old hands. Bibi cuddled near the old lady. So much had changed since that day Bibi left her home. In the pastures of Mother K she had found peace and Allah. In the pains of Uzaid's childbirth she found humility and purpose.

She had grown pompous and defensive with Zaman. He did not understand how putting on weight had made her feel ugly and less of a woman and a person. She did not like her own body. For a while she blamed her pregnancy and the baby, but she knew that was silly. She needed Zaman to understand and help her. She tried to get back at him. She did not want to wear the Islamic clothes she knew he admired and wanted her to wear. She had promised him to wear the scarf on her head but she never did. She had even stopped praying to get him angry. So much had gone wrong.

She had too much weight and a new baby and noone to tell her how to manage. Her parents and family had migrated to the USA since she was three months with Uzaid. Her only friend and relative was old Aunty Khairool who was an old cousin of her father's parents. Now Bibi was only 125 pounds. All the bad weight was gone. Her hair was long past her waist. She was regular with her fasts and her prayers. She only wore the Islamic long clothes and kept her hair covered. Losing weight had also changed her voice and over the years she had acquired an American accent which usually happened to immigrants living in the USA. She was a new person. She had passed the test. Her own husband and daughter had not recognized her. But what was next Bibi wondered. Fate had made her friends with her mother-in-law. What would happen if they knew who she really was? Bibi decided to put it all away from her for a while. She was happy and safe at this cottage. She needed time to unwind and be herself. It was her first vacation in forever. Bibi dried her tears and smiled. She was going to eat, run, play and be a girl again as much as was allowed.

She had long hot days and cool long nights. She heard herself laugh and let her hair get tangled in the tropical breeze. She ran barefoot behind chickens and sheep. She was barely 32. The years and responsibilities had sometimes made her feel like 50. In Mother K's cottage, she felt like sixteen. It was a hot Friday. Bibi sat on a small bench under the house. She was surprised at the way Uzaid adapted to life. He had gone through nine Summers and Winters and Springs and yet he was so happy running with Chico to feed the cows and helping Grandma K with milking. He drank the milk straight from the milking like Mother K. Bibi watched him climb the giant mango trees and the clustered sapodilla bark while

Chico stood at the root and barked and barked. Chico wished he could climb too. They went fishing in the dark waters of the 'backdam' for sweet bony houri fish and prehistoric hassar. Bibi treated herself to daily bellyful of sweet cool coconut water and delicious white coconut jelly from the hundreds of trees all around.

That weekend after a week of fun, Bibi had to do washing. The sun was very bright and very hot. Aunty K would always say, "Don't waste the good sunshine, put some clothes on the line." Washing the clothes by hand in MotherK's big tub was an adventure. Bibi had 'soaked' them in the soapy water since she got up for Fajr. Now at 9.00am as Senor Sun was beginning to really wake up, Bibi got her clothes pins and bucket and clothes basket and set to work. Each garment was taken by parts and held by one hand and scrubbed over itself by the other hand. It was hard work for the heel of the palm of both hands. After each piece was washed, it was wrung by tight twisting by the hands and then placed in a basket. Uzaid had fun taking the soapy water to blow bubbles and Chico ran after them to catch them but they melted or turned to nothing and Chico could not understand where they went. When the clothes were all 'screeched', the tub was emptied into the drains and Uzaid helped his mom refill the tub with clean water from a huge tank in the yard fetching the water by buckets. The soapy clothes were then rinsed and wrung and put into the clothes basket. Bibi was wearing a soft pants and a small tee shirt to do the washing outside. She took her basket to the long lines in the sunshine. It was hard work reaching tall lines but the sun and the wind felt pure and good. Bibi took her time pinning her clothes on the line. She sang to herself as she worked.

CHAPTER SIX

Zaman at the Cottage

Zaman stopped in front of the cottage but he did not get out of his van. He looked at the billowing sheets and other things on the lines and he looked at the pretty girl with long black hair. She was fair and small. He could see the skin of her waist every time she tip toed to pin the clothes. She was singing but he could not hear what she was singing. Zaman smiled, a thing he did not do very often. From the first instant, he was attracted to this girl. He blamed his thoughts and memories of Naj for that. Since his sleepness night, he thought every woman he saw could be Naj. Every fat woman, every skinny girl, could be Naj. Even this tip toeing singer looked familiar. But Zaman blinked his eyes. How silly could he get. What was he doing to himself. His Naj was a rebel. She could not wear long clothes and cover her hair and she hated glasses and how could a 200 pound ever be reduced to half that size. "Stop dreaming Zaman", he told himself. People had the same features, all the world was a family and this little nurse was off limits but she still made Zaman smile.

He waited until she got back inside the house and then he honked his horn and got out of the van and walked towards the cottage. He called out his Salaam. Chico was already bounding out to see who the strange voice was. He sat back barking. Uzaid followed and rushed out when he saw Zaman and hugged the surprised man around his waist. "Hi Uncle Zaman, nice to see you here", the child said in sincere greeting.

Zaman laughed and looked at Chico. The dog looked unsure of letting Zaman go any further. He saw Uzaid hug the stranger and Uzaid said to him, "Its okay Chico, he is family, he is Uncle Zaman". Zaman spoke gently to Guard General Chico and slowly put out his hand and patted the dog's head. Chico wagged his tail. "There you go", Zaman said and he confidently moved past to get to the hammock.

Uzaid went inside to tell his mom that there was visitor. Bibi had heard Zaman's voice and her body reacted with a happiness and intense nervous fright at the same time. She was still wearing wet pants and tee shirt. She had to get dressed. Why was he here? Bibi looked at Mother K who had heard the dog barking and was aware that Zaman was waiting. "Its him!" Bibi whispered, "please go see what he wants." Mother Khairool got her walking stick and leaning on it she walked out to answer Zaman. "Assalamualaikum", he said as Mother K appeared. "My mother is not well and she asked me to get Bibi." "Waalaikumassalam", Aunty K said in her gruffest voice. "How did you find us?" she asked Zaman. He laughed. "Bibi left the directions with Mom and everyone around knows you Aunty K." Uzaid was waiting impatiently to talk to Zaman. "Uncle, did you pick the tomatoes? What are you picking tomorrow?" he asked. "Can I come help pick cucumbers?" Zaman laughed at the child's enthusiasm. "You will have to ask your mother. Where is she?" "Are we going back with you", the boy persisted. Mother K put an arm out to Uzaid in a motion of caution and then she went back inside to Bibi. Zaman leaned against a wooden support of the house and waited. He talked to Uzaid answering the boy's questions about the farm and explaining about his mother not being well. Zaman had not been in much contact or conversation with Bibi. She did not stay around him and he thought she was probably shy. This impressed and amused him. Women living and working in New York were usually aggressive and open. This little Bibi was an interesting case. She bothered him in a good way. She came to the door fully dressed in a long brown gown and a patterned cream silk scarf on her hair and dark prescription shades. She smelled of freshness, just out of the bath and floral sweetness. Zaman stopped playing in his mind and became serious. He leaned off the post and looked to the ground as she spoke. She gave him salaam and asked in eagerness and concern about Maimoona. When she learned that Mai was having problems with her movement again, Bibi was worried. Mai could be having a stroke. She needed to get to a hospital. Bibi collected her Nurse's Bag and explained to Mother K that she had to go check on Maimoona. "Are you sure you would be alright?" the old lady asked. Bibi understood the question. She was not sure, but she had to see Mai. Bibi did not want to take Uzaid with her. She needed the time to look after Maimoona. He was upset when She told him to stay with Mother K.

Chico sensed his mood and came to him and barked and nuzzled his hand. He then sat at Uzaid's feet and looked up at him. The two had become good friends. Uzaid could not stay angry very long. He rubbed the dog's head and asked permission to go pick mangoes out back. Bibi looked at Mother K and she told Uzaid to go. He waved to the three grown ups and left with his faithful Chico. Bibi rode in a back seat of the spacious van. She did not talk to Zaman while he was driving. He too was very quiet. He was worried about his mother. He did not realize until Bibi explained, how seriously ill she could be.

CHAPTER SEVEN

Bibi and the Abdools

Maimoona looked pale and her blood pressure was fifty points higher than was safe. She had not taken her medicines in two days and she had not slept much she said. Bibi wanted her to go to the hospital but Mai said all she needed was some good sleep. Bibi gave her the tablets she should have taken and massaged her hands and feet gently until she fell asleep. She left quietly and opened the door a little so that she could hear if Mai called. Zaman was waiting around outside the door. Bibi went down the stairs to the kitchen. He followed her. She was angry. Maimoona was the picture of neglect in a home with a grown son and an agile grand daughter. "What happened here?" Bibi asked. "What has upset her so much? How come she has not had her medicine in two days?" Bibi knew to him she was a stranger in the home but she and Mai had gone through illness and lived together. She cared for the busy body grand mother and above it all though it could not now be known, Mai was her mother-in-law, grandmother of her children. Zaman put his hands in his pocket and started to walk away. It was personal. It was private. How could he explain. He could feel Bibi watching him walk away. She would get her answers from Mai when she awoke. He did not like conversations with females who began with accusations, even implied as these were. But he had to answer her. She needed to know for his mother's sake. "Mother and Salma are not getting along." "They had a tussle last evening. Mother said Sal was rude and she was going to switch her. She actually did give her a red sting on her feet and Salma pushed her and Mai fell." Zaman related the incident in a 'because he was asked' tone.

Bibi sat in a chair in the kitchen. "Ya Allah!" she exclaimed. "I am sorry!" she said quietly, suddenly feeling the guilt of a runaway mother. "Mai needs to rest. I will check her vitals when she is up. I still think she should go to the hospital," Bibi told Zaman. "How long will you be staying?" he asked. "I am not sure," Bibi told him. "If it is okay I would like to stay with her tonight and go with her to the hospital tomorrow Inshallah." Zamam shrugged his shoulders. "If you need anything let me know," she heard him say as he walked up the stairs to his room at the end of the hall. Bibi was tired from the washing at Mother K's but she could not rest. It was early afternoon. There was no Salma in view and Bibi did not want to go knocking on her door. The child was going through some major issues and Bibi felt helpless just looking on. The kitchen was a good place to get busy in. Bibi started cleaning and cooking. She made chicken barley soup for Maimoona and she put a cake in the big oven. She seasoned some portions of the chicken for stove top roasting and decided to make potato salad to complement the chicken and added chunky slices of garlic bread to the oven. She was peeling the potatoes over the sink when she was interrupted by Miss Salma Abdool.

Bibi looked up as the voice said, "Hi! Assalamualaikum." Bibi replied as she should but did not encourage further conversation. Salma opened the refrigerator and stood for a while deciding. She finally closed the door with her feet as she took a can of soda and an old half sandwich out. Bibi continued peeling her potatoes. She could feel the teen sizing her up. "What kind of cake you making?" the girl asked. "Its orange pound cake", Bibi answered. "Oh! I like chocolate cake," Salma retorted. Bibi made no response. When the sandwich and soda were noisily finished, the child asked, "What is wrong with Grandma?" Bibi smiled. There was a heart in all that anger after all. Without looking up from her potatoes Bibi told her, "Something has upset your Grandmother very much and it made her blood pressure very high. It can affect her heart again." Salma listened and then said, "Oh!" Bibi washed the potaoes and opened cans of corn and peas and carrots for the salad. Salma watched and Bibi waited for the next question. "You married?" Salma asked. Bibi nearly dropped the can of peas. "Yes I am," she answered. "Oh!" Salma said again. It was a happier Oh. "So why he didn't come with you?" Salma asked again. "He had to work," Bibi lied. Somehow the knowledge that Bibi was married with a husband was good for Salma. She came into the kitchen and asked to help. Bibi watched and went along with the drama. The hours went quickly. Mai was up and Bibi ate dinner with her in her room. She could hear Salma laughing with Zaman downstairs as they ate in the kitchen. Good food was always good. It brought laughter to the house tonight.

Bibi smiled as she cleared up the dishes later. The girl who only liked chocolate cake almost finished the orange pound cake. Zaman and Salma and Maimoona were all asleep by 9.00pm. Bibi said her night prayers and checked on Mai. Her blood pressure was okay but she had a fever and her forehead was sweaty. Bibi decided to sleep in the living room at the foot of the stairs so she could hear if Maimoona awoke during the night and called. She dusted the comfortable familiar old sofa and stretched out. Her hair hang over the hand rest of the chair as she freed it from the scarf. She covered with a small shawl and picked up the day's newspaper. She read the headlines and tiredness claimed her senses. She was soon asleep. Zaman had eaten too much chicken and potato salad. It was good food but it had made him sleepy and he went to bed without praying his Esha salaat. His watch said 1.30am in the dark morning of a new day. He walked to his mother's room because the door was slightly open and he looked in. She was snoring quietly. He came out and looked down the stairs at the two small white feet sticking out from under a shawl. He realized that Bibi had left Maimoona's door open so he left it the same way.

He moved to go to the bathroom upstairs but instead he stood at the top of the stairs looking at the sleeping nurse. Her feet looked familiar to him. He remembered small feet like that with golden anklets lying on the same sofa, it was Naj, the first week of their marriage. Zaman shook his head free of his memories and imagination and got quietly angry. He hurried to make his wudu to pray the salaat he missed.

Bibi was awakened by the movement upstairs. She tied her hair up and put her scarf back on. She went to check on Mai. The fever was worse. Bibi applied a cool cloth to wipe the sweating neck and head.

Mai was still asleep. It was 2.00am. The alarm was set for 4.30am for the Fajr prayer. Bibi needed to sleep some more. She curled up at the foot of the big king sized bed across from Mai and continued her beauty rest.

Morning came quickly. Maimoona was not well. She made to fuss or objection as Bibi got her ready to go to the hospital. Bibi's worries were confirmed. Mai had to remain in the hospital so stress tests could be done. She was there for a whole week.

Bibi found herself alone at home with Zaman very often. They did not speak more than what was necessary but locked in her room she was very aware of him three doors away. She missed him. He looked more mature in his slightly graying hair and thick beard. He was a hairy man but she loved it and she loved him.

Uzaid and her training and her two jobs kept her busy the last ten years. She thought of herself as his wife and maintained a status of married to all who tried to make advances. Her Muslim attire was an outward expression of her as a Muslim and in the USA to be Muslim was like being an enemy of the state or being judged as a terrorist. Bibi dwelled peacefully and was kind to those around her. She had no problems with anyone in the USA. She did not agree with the suicide bombings of the Muslims in the Middle East. It was not stated in the Quran that innocent lives could be taken for others. It was also not a blessed act to take one's own life. However it was allowed to defend one's family and home and Muslim territory from invasion and persecution. Bibi always said a prayer for the Muslims and non Muslims around the world. Most times the killing and dissention seemed senseless. All problems could be solved by going to the Quran or checking the Sunnah of Prophet Muhammad(May Allah be pleased with him). Bibi did not involve herself in these issues at any high forum. She prayed for Peace and understanding. She prayed for Guidance for the Ummah of Muhammad(May Allah be pleased with him)

Bibi had her own set of problems she was praying about. She had taken three months off from work to come back home. What did she hope to achieve? She didn't think it through, but something had to happen. Zaman was still her husband. They had both made mistakes but it was different now. He had a son he did not know was his son. She had neglected a daughter for ten years. How could she just walk back into their lives. They had never bothered to find her or try to make things right. These thoughts went back and forth in Bibi's head.

Suppose they did not forgive her. Suppose they all turned on her, Maimoona, Zaman, Salma and even Uzaid. Bibi could lose all. She was scared. Maybe she should take her son and go back to New York she thought. But Bibi knew she couldn't. She could not walk out on Salma again. Somehow she had to be friend the child.

Zaman lay on his bed thinking. He was attracted to the pretty nurse. He wondered what her real story was. Maimoona said there was no husband but Salma said there was one in New York. There was no mail being received or sent and there were no urgent phone calls. This pretty nurse was alone. Zaman smiled and then stopped himself. He thought about Naj. She had been gone ten years. She was probably married somewhere. But Zaman knew he did not really think that. One day Naj would come back. She left on her own. She would come back on her own. He didn't know how he felt about Naj. She was Salma's mother. Zaman loved her very much once and he knew she loved him. How could a woman walk away for ten years? That question was often in his mind. She had family in the USA but he did not think it was right for him to go finding Naj. She walked out. She had to come back. Then he would know what had to be done. Zaman opened his door and made his way down the stairs. Bibi was in the kitchen singing. She quickly stopped when she saw him. He got some juice and went to the living room. The song was familiar. Was it the song or the voice singing it? It was a Muslim children's lullaby Naj used to sing to Salma. Zaman did not think about it any more. It had to be a coincidence. Many people sang that same song to their children.

They got through the week with good news. Maimoona had slight blockage of her arteries which was treatable at the hospital. Her blood cholesterol was above the safe limit, so she got medication for that. With good care and rest, she was okay for many more years, so the doctors said. Everyone was happy. Maimoona was glad to be back home.

CHAPTER EIGHT

A Child is Missing

January had moved into February. Bibi had returned to Aunty Khairool but she made weekly checks on Mai. Time was going and decisions had to be made. Mai did not talk of going back to New York. Bibi was praying and praying for an answer as to what course her life must take. February brought rain. Zaman tried to save his lettuce and cabbages from flooding. It was a challenge every year. Sometimes he reaped before the downpours and sometimes he lost some. The weather was the plan and will of Allah. Salma was busy with school. She had final examinations in June. She would then be graduating from high school. She kept good grades and worked hard. She wanted to do well. She wanted to enter a good college and train as a Mathematics teacher. The school had offered free extra classes in English Language and Mathematics. Zaman allowed her to take the classes. One rainy Friday, Bibi and Uzaid took the long ride to Maimoona's. It was 5.00pm. They were packed to stay overnight. Mai opened the door. She was worried. Something was not right she said. Zaman had left at 4.00pm to get Salma from classes. They were not yet back. Bibi tried to calm the worried grandmother. Darkness came early and more darkness. It was 7.00pm. Zaman came back wet and defeated. He did not announce this to everyone. In answer to Maimoona's eager queries, he told them all that Salma was staying with her aunt Asma. They all knew that the doctors had made Asma rest in the last month of her seventh pregnancy. Now Maimoona turned her concern to Asma. She wondered if all was well with her.

The excitement and wondering was not good for Mai's health. Bibi gave her extra blood pressure and heart medication to have her sleep soundly all night. She took the fussing lady up the stairs to her room and did not leave her until she was calm and tucked in and going to sleep. Bibi hurried down the stairs to Zaman pacing the living room. She had a mother's, wife's and woman's intuition, he did not tell them the truth. She did not allow him to hedge, she asked quite clearly and seriously yet quietly enough that Uzaid could not hear, "What happened?" He was in anguish, his eyes were red and tired. "I cant find her," she heard him say. He told her about the boy Salma liked and his fears concerning that. Bibi's heart beat faster and her mouth was dry. She was scared for her child. She asked if he had checked the boy's house or the house of his friends or the homes of Salma's friends. Zaman had checked most of the friends. Classes had been cancelled that day. Children were sent home since 2.00pm because of the very bad weather. It was after 8.00pm going on nine. Bibi was shaking inside. Zaman said he had to go out again. He had to find her. Uzaid surprised them both by insisting to go too. He had heard enough to know that Salma was missing. "Please Mummy", he begged, "I can help to look while Uncle Zaman is driving."

Bibi hesitated but the child insisted. She looked at him and the voluntary way he reacted. Salma was his sister. He had every right to want to help. The common blood could not be denied though the child did not know it. Together they left in Zaman's van.

Bibi stood at the window and watched them drive away. Her legs were shaky and her hands were cold. She cried aloud from her heart. Her whole family was in that rain. "Please my Creator, please let them be alright!" she begged. She made wudu and went to her prayer rug. Only Allah could help. He was the All Seeing and All Knowing One. He knew where Salma was. He would guide Zaman. Bibi did two rakaats of salaat crying throughout. She then brought her hands up for duaa. "Ya Allah! I praise Thee by that name by which you are most pleased. I praise Thee by that name with which you answer Duaas, Oh my Allah, I send salaam to Prophet Muhammad, may you be pleased with him and may he intercede for us on the Day of Qiyamaat. Please Oh Allah, please cover my children, cover Salma and Uzaid and please cover my husband. Please forgive us the things in our life that displease you and please give us a chance at a new life." Bibi continued praising Allah by his Glorious Names and she put her face in her cupped palms and kept crying. "Please let Salma be safe, please let Salma be safe," she begged.

Zaman found Zaid and his friends in a Pools bar. He beat them all up. They laughed when he asked for his daughter and Zaman could only reply with his fist. He lashed out at the four youths gathered around a Pools table. The Manager for the place was shouting for order but everyone stepped back when they saw the purpose on Zaman's face. "Where is she?" he asked Zaid. The boy laughed and Zaman was enraged. He grabbed and he pounded. The boys hit him too but he did not feel anything. He wanted answers. One boy took out a knife and swiped Zaman as he got close. It caught him across the abdomen and enraged him more. He was chasing them around the table and around the chairs of the small bar. He got hold of Zaid again and started choking him. "Tell me what you did. Where is she?" he asked. The boy denied even knowing such a person. Zaman squeezed harder and the youth's legs got weak. His friends tried to grab Zaman's arms and save their friend. Finally one boy shouted. "Let the Man go. We didn't do anything. We left her at the school!" Zaman let the boy fall to the floor.

Zaid raised his hand to his throat and coughed. His friends went to help him. He knew Zaman would have killed him.

Uzaid was ordered to stay in the van but he saw all that happened in the Bar. When Zaman got back to the van he was breathing heavily and blood had soaked his shirt and his pants. He put the van in gear, backed out and got unto the road headed for the High School. It was a simple two storied old wooden building. The gates were locked. Zaman drove right through them to the locked front doors. He got out in the pouring rain. The van's lights showed the way to the doors. Zaman kicked them in and walked through the quiet rooms calling for Salma. There was noone in the school. Uzaid could see tears down Zaman's face. Wherever he walked turned red as blood seeped down his feet. He had been cut deep across his lower abdomen. Zaman came back out through the school doors and fell on his knees on the water swirling around the van. He bowed his head in his hands and cried out. "Oh Allah! Oh Allah! Please, please! Please let me find her."

Zaid took a flash light from the van and got out. He watched Zaman on his knees in the rain. Zaid decided to walk around the school to the back where there was a big field. He shone the light and called for Salma. It was cold and the child was quickly soaked to his skin. He turned to go and pointed his light to the small cycle shed at the back of the school and another small storage shed for building materials. He heard a sound. It was like the whine of a hurt dog. He shone the light through the latticed door and into two frightened black eyes. He looked again and realized it was a head, it was Salma crouched with her legs up and teeth chattering. "Oh my God!" Uzaid said in surprise and happiness and he dropped the light and tried to open the shed. The door was already open and he reached Salma and sat next to her and hugged her. After a minute he got her up and they walked out. He picked up the light and took her to the van. "Where is Dad?" she stammered. Uzaid called out for Zaman. There was no answer. Salma screamed as she saw her father collapsed in front of the vehicle. She ran to him calling, "Dad! Dad!" She tried to pull him up, right where he was cut. When she saw the blood she started screaming more. Zaman opened his eyes and called her name and he was unconscious again. "I am here Dad. I am alright!" Salma said as she cried. Zaman was hurt and weak. The children pulled him and helped each other get him into the back seat of the van. Salma climbed into the driver's seat. Uzaid was seated across from her and he looked aghast. "You are going to drive?" he asked. "I don't have a license but Dad taught me to drive the tractor on the farm and we have to get home," she told him as she shifted the gears and they reversed too quickly out of the school yard. They saw no one else on the road and very soon they came to a halt in their own driveway.

CHAPTER NINE

Patient Zaman

Despite her years of training and working as a nurse, when Bibi saw the two children pulling a pale and bloody Zaman, she screamed. Zaman was heavy and they could not get him upstairs. Thank God, Bibi thought, that they had built the self contained room downstairs when she was pregnant with Salma. They finally got Zaman unto the big bed. Bibi hugged Salma and kissed her and said to her, "I am glad you are safe". She then told her to go up and shower and change into dry clothes but first she had to get clean clothes for her father. Uzaid got a hug and he was instructed to see that the doors were locked and he was to get cleaned up and check on the sleeping Grandmother but first he had to get Bibi's Nurse's bag from upstairs. Both children left to do as asked. Bibi was alone with her husband. She felt for his pulse. It was weak but he was alive. Quickly and as gently as she could, she took all his clothes off and placed them in a big plastic pail. With hot water and antiseptic, she cleaned the wound. She kept supplies of most things needed in a hospital in her bag. She gave him shots for numbing the pain and with catgut she tried her best with small quick stitches to sew him up. None of his internal organs was damaged. It was an across the abdomen half inch flesh wound. He had lost a lot of blood. She cleaned him up and gave him a shot to sleep.

Salma had showered and changed and watched as Bibi looked after her Dad. Salma looked at the pale exhausted face as he lay on the bed.

She made this happen to him. Uzaid told her everything about the fight at the Bar. She was happy that her Dad had nearly killed Zaid and he had beat up his friends. But the child could not stop crying as she looked at her Dad. Bibi assured her that Zaman would soon be well again.

As they left Zaman to rest, Bibi took the exhausted Salma to the living room and hugged her while she cried. After a while as she stroked the child's hair in a soothing way, she asked softly, "Do you want to tell me?" Salma leaned against the warmth of Bibi. "Nothing happened! Nothing happened," the child said. "He wanted to do things. He was pulling at me and pushing me but I ran away. I ran away to the back and hid in the shed. I was afraid his friends would find me." Bibi looked up to the heavens and said "Alhamdulilah!" quietly. She believed the child.

It was a long night. Bibi thanked Allah over and over. She watched Salma and Uzaid playing scrabble on the living room floor at 1.30am in the morning.

Uzaid had felt the urge to protect Salma, never bothering to understand or explain it. He wanted to tease Salma since their first meeting for her haughtiness. He was sorry for her. He was so happy when he found her and he was proud to see the way she helped with her Dad and the way she drove them home in that rain. Uzaid was glad they were all together and okay and he was beating her at scrabble. He had just played the word 'sequestered' from triple to triple earning himself 126 points.

Bibi walked slowly up the stairs to check on Maimoona. She was still asleep. Her blood pressure was okay. Her heart rate was good. She had slept through the crisis. Bibi was grateful.

She went back down the stairs to Zaman's room. She sat at the edge of the big bed. It was larger than a king size made especially for her when she was pregnant with Salma. How much had happened on that bed. Bibi looked at the tired face of her husband. She loved to play with his beard and massage his tired feet. She wanted everything to be okay. She wished he would open his eyes and she would give salaam and say, I am sorry I left in a hurry. I am back. And life would go on. She still loved him so much. But, she had kept a son from him. She had kept a sister from her son. Bibi was tired. She did not want to think of all the wrong that had been done. Was it possible that they could go on? Did

Zaman still love her? Would he take her back? Would he trust her? Bibi went over to the side of the bed where he was. She stroked his beard. It was dry. It needed olive oil to soften it and make it brighter. She passed her hands through his thick curly hair. He was sweating. She checked his temperature. He had a fever. It was because of all the cold rain he had been soaked in. Nurse Bibi got a small towel and cool water from the tap. She gently cooled his forehead and his upper arms. He was calling names. He called for Salma over and over. Bibi soothed his brow and his hair and sang a lullaby as she tried to calm him in his delirious state. She ran the soft pad of her fingers down his arms and his neck and his chest through the mass of soft hair and down to his feet. He was her Big Baby. She used to call him that. As she traced the muscles of his feet she could feel him relax and go into a deep sleep. She gave him more antibiotic and pain killer shots on his hip and rear. She then sat at the foot of the bed and put her hands on his feet. They were callused and hard from the farm work. Bibi sat there massaging her husband's feet. She squeezed and rubbed for a long time. Then she walked back to the head of the bed and kissed her husband lightly on the lips. She closed the door gently and left.

Salma was getting very sleepy. So much had happened that day and Uzaid had beaten her at scrabble by 200points. She was still shaken by it all and she needed sleep. She saw Bibi leave to check on Grandma and then come down to check on Zaman. Salma walked to the downstairs suite to peep in on her Dad. She heard a voice singing a lullaby. Many nights she had imagined hearing it. She was afraid it was the things of the spirit world coming to haunt her. She stood by the half closed door and peeped into the room. It was Bibi singing to her father. Salma watched her cooling his forehead and playing with his hair. Salma could not move. Why was Bibi doing these things? Could this be her mother? Was her mother a pretty nurse? For a while Salma was happy at the thought. But her mother had left her. Her mother had left her alone with her Dad. He had grown old and tired. Bibi said she had a husband in New York. Was she married again and was Uzaid, Salma's half brother?

Salma 's sleepy brain was thinking all these things and she was getting angry. If Bibi was married, why did she come back to their lives? How could she come back to hurt them again? Then Salma saw Bibi kiss

Zaman. The confused child tip toe away from the room and up the stairs to her room. She sat on her bed to think about what she had seen and heard. Why would Bibi kiss her father if she was married to someone else? Maybe she still loved Zaman. Could Bibi really be her mother? Salma knew that voice and that lullaby. Noone else could sing like that. Salma knew she was glad Bibi was there tonight. She would always remember Uzaid's face when he found her. She felt connected to these people. She did not want any bad things happening. Zaman had taught his little girl to pray. It was one of those times when Salma needed to have a serious sincere conversation with Allah. She made her Wudu and stood on the prayer rug in a corner of her room. She did two rakaats of Salaat and bowed her head to the floor and cried her little frightened heart out. "Oh my Allah", she cried, "You saved me today. You saved me from shame. You gave me the strength to run away from that boy. I knew it was wrong and you guided me rightly. Please forgive me for encouraging him. Forgive me for staying back to be with him. I did not want to do bad things Oh Allah. I thought he was nice and he ...." She stopped speaking and continued crying. She then sat up and cupped her palms in front of her and prayed some more. "Oh my Allah, I am so glad you gave Dad the strength to beat up those boys. Please don't let Dad be angry with me. Please forgive me Oh Allah. Please forgive me. Please help me to finish my studies and do well. Please save me from evil people and evil things."

As she sat there thinking about her life and all that had happened, Salma added more to her duaa with Allah. "Please Oh Allah, help me to understand who Bibi and Uzaid are in our lives. Please dont let them upset our lives. Please don't let them upset Dad. Please watch over our home and watch over us," she concluded as the tiredness made her yawn. She got up and got ready for bed.

CHAPTER TEN

Finding out things

Bibi found Uzaid already asleep on the sofa. He was too heavy to take upstairs and she did not want to awaken him. She covered him and let him sleep. Bibi went to the kitchen and sat at the small table there. It had been a long day and a crazy night and now a new day was almost dawning. Bibi warmed some chamomile tea and sipped it. It was almost 4.30am, time for the morning Fajr prayer. She prepared for salaat and stood on her prayer rug in a corner of the living room. She took her time with the closing duaa. She thanked Allah all the while for saving Zaman and Salma. She begged for Allah's forgiveness and especially begged for His Guidance. She then got up and took off her scarf. Her body was tired tired. She curled up in the recliner next to the sofa and was soon asleep.

Habit got Zaman up at 4.45am. He felt the sting across his body. He reached down with his arm and hit the stitches and winced with pain. He saw the blackness of the night give way to the white light of dawn. He tried to sit up. He felt relaxed all over. He had a good sleep. Then he tried to remember the events of the past night.

He knew they found Salma and there was rain. How did he get home and why was he in the downstairs suite. It had to be Bibi who stitched him up and he remembered soft hands in his hair. Zaman smiled and passed his hands through his own hair. It must have been a dream he thought. He tried to stand at the side of the bed but his head was dizzy from the loss of blood. He had to get to the bathroom. Slowly he made his way and relieved himself. He then washed and prepared for the Fajr salaat. He would have to sit on the chair next to the bed to pray but he did not want to ignore his salaat. It took some time but he finished praying and made his duaa to Allah. He then ventured slowly out of the room holding a pillow to his cut abdomen. He saw Uzaid on the sofa and Bibi curled up in his recliner, her long black hair falling over the sides. Something drew him to that girl but he kept pulling himself away. He heard a noise upstairs and remembered Maimoona. He wondered if she knew of the busy night they had. Bibi said she would sleep until morning. Zaman made his way up the stairs using the rails for support. The stitches burned everytime he raised his legs to step.

Maimoona was up. She was on her prayer rug reading her Quran. Zaman looked in and smiled at her. She smiled back in acknowledgement and continued her reading. Zaman looked in on Salma. She had been crying. He could see the red nose and she was snoring. He stroked her hair. She was his baby girl. Only Allah knew how he felt when he could not find her. He was so glad she was in her bed safe at home. He silently prayed that nothing had happened last night and she was okay. As Zaman made his way to his room upstairs, he passed the slightly open door of Bibi's room. He was curious. His feet walked right in. What was he looking for? He didn't know? It was not like him to search through people's belongings but he was peeping into drawers without thinking. He saw Bibi's handbag on her bed. He listened for movement in the house. He heard no noise so he emptied the ladies purse unto the bed. There was perfume and lipstick and eye shadow. Zaman smiled. The Nurse liked to dress up. He was just mischievous he thought. Why was he doing this? But he did not stop. He flipped through her address book. There was nothing interesting there. Then he saw the two passports. Wow! He did not realize that the Nurse and her son were American citizens. It was an involuntary gesture to flip through the pages of the passport to see where the good Nurse traveled . . . and to look at her picture. Zaman was smiling at the young face that looked back at him. He was impressed. Bibi had taken out her American Citizen passport photographs with her Islamic scarf on her head. He was really impressed. He then read the name under the photograph. Mrs Najma Abdool, status, married, date of birth, July 7th. He looked again. Did he read that correctly. He looked at the photograph. Mrs Najma Abdool. He read it again. What sick joke was this.

He then opened the second passport he found. He looked down at the baby face of Uzaid. The name was, Uzaid Abdool, Mother, Najma Abdool, Father, Zaman Abdool. The child was born on Jan 9th. Zaman turned the passports over and over and looked at the names. He did not know whether to be so happy or angry at being fooled. Uzaid was his son. This girl was his Naj. How could this be? Zaman stared at the faces before him. He heard his mother calling. Zaman quickly put the things back into the bag and pushed it under the pillow of the bed. He slipped out of the room and went to check on his mother. Maimoona liked to pray and blow her blessings on her son. Zaman held a hand to his abdomen, glad that he wore the big teeshirt to cover himself. His mother would be too worried if she saw the stitches. He told her he had stomach cramps and he was sick during the night and the children and Bibi were up with him. Maimoona began to fuss. She knew just what he needed and she was going downstairs to the kitchen to get a herbal concoction to give him a good cleansing. Zaman tried to tell her not to bother but Maimoona had purpose for the day and she made her way down the stairs. She saw Uzaid on the Sofa and Bibi on the recliner. It was strange seeing them like that asleep. She wondered what really happened last night. It was her chance to get breakfast for them. Bibi was always busy looking after everyone. Mai was happy to get things done in the kitchen.

Zaman walked quietly down the stairs after his mother and went back to his bed in the downstairs suite. He fixed himself as he found himself when he awoke. The exertion of the morning had made him tired and dizzy. He was sweating and exhausted. He swung his legs up gently and lay back on the big pillows.

His head was filled with questions. How could Bibi be Naj? How did she lose all the weight? How did she become such a good Muslim? Was it all an act? She must have had men in her life in ten years. Was Uzaid really his son? Did she really meet his mother by chance? How could she come to his home? What did she want? Zaman was confused. He was waiting all the time for Naj to come back but she had come back and he did not even know. He was not prepared. He did not know what to do. His eyes closed as his exhausted body slept.

CHAPTER ELEVEN

A Nurse is Fooled

Bibi was awakened by the sound of cracking eggs. She roused quickly on seeing the sun so brightly up. It was 7.30am. Uzaid was still stretched out on the sofa. She saw Maimoona in the kitchen. "Assalamualaikum, What you doing?" she asked. "I am making breakfast this morning", Mai told her. "You get cleaned up, the pancakes are almost done." Bibi laughed. She did not protest. The Grandmother was happy, that was best for all. Bibi went up the stairs to use the facilities and quickly showered and changed. She put on a new gown and scarf and searched for her bag with her perfume and make up. She found it hidden under the pillows. The children must have put it there when she sent them to get her Nurse's bag last night she thought. She made herself presentable and said her morning prayers and then went down to join Maimoona in the kitchen. The coffee was great, the eggs were fluffy and the pancakes were light. "Homemade syrup!" Mai declared proudly as she poured more unto Bibi's plate. Bibi sat there trying to find a way to explain the night's events to Maimoona. She was sure the old lady had questions. Bibi decided to wait until she was asked. She was going to enjoy every bite of breakfast, then worry about the new day. Before they were done there was a caller at the door. It was Shaheed, Asma's husband. He was nervous and scared. Asma had started getting pains for the baby and the village midwife had advised them to get to a hospital. The baby was in a breach position. Asma wanted her mother.

Grandma Mai had dealt with a breach birth with her son Zaheer. Asma was in the car and Shaheed stood at the door. Maimoona got up and took her apron off. Bibi looked up at her. "I have to go with her." Mai said. "I will be alright. I will be in a hospital." "Okay", Bibi said and she walked her to the door and to the car where Asma lay in contractions in the back seat. She watched them drive off and walked back inside. It was all quiet. Bibi tidied the kitchen and went to check on Zaman. He needed to eat and take more antibiotics. She checked his stitches. They looked red and disturbed. Maybe he had turned during the night. She checked his forehead and his neck. He had no fever. Zaman lay there fully aware of her. Her hands were soft and gentle. She smelled fresh and sweet. She was putting out the antibiotics and painkillers he had to take. As she moved away to part the thick curtains slightly, he coughed and tried to sit up. She hurried to his side saying, "No, No." as he put a hand to his abdomen. She spoke softly and gave him salaam. He answered in tones of pain and exhaustion. "Can you go to the bathroom?" he heard her say. He let her see him try and then leaned on her for support as she took him across the room to the bathroom. He said he was going to be alright. She left him and went to the kitchen to get him breakfast. She brought it all back on a tray at put it on a table beside his bed.

Zaman looked very weak and barely able to get back into bed. He lay in a half sitting position and seemed unable to feed himself. "Please help me", he whispered to the Nurse. Bibi was glad to. She fed him soup and pieces of toast. She gave him sweet cool papaya by the spoonful and wiped his mouth. She took the tray back to the kitchen and returned to put his tablets on his tongue and hold the glass to his lips so he could drink the cool water. "You need to rest," she told him. He agreed with a nod and leaned back on the pillows and closed his eyes. Bibi looked at him as he lay there. He looked very weak. Maybe he had lost more blood than she thought. He might have to rest all week. She smoothed the sheets and left. Zaman opened his eyes and smiled. He was exhausted but not that weak and it felt good to be pampered by the good Nurse.

Asma had a baby boy. There was news of how Maimoona shifted the child so he could be born. It was a Mother's hands of faith and love versus science and medicine. Mai then went home with Asma to help her and fuss over a houseful of Grandchildren. Meanwhile, Zaman was recovering but slowly it seems. He could be heard playing and laughing with Salma and Uzaid but he still needed help with eating and moving. Bibi had spent many afternoons massaging his feet and head as he claimed he had cramps and bad headaches. But Bibi knew she was being fooled. The stitches were healing very quickly and Zaman did not need her help but Bibi played along and she liked attending to him.

Zaman was planning with the children. Since the night of the attack, Salma had let him know what she had seen Bibi do to him in his room. Zaman easily explained to his daughter that, "Your Mummy is home." He then told Uzaid that he was his son. He told them both not to judge their mother since it was grown-up business and misunderstanding that had put them apart. They were all together now. The children had no regrets. Uzaid thought it was "cool", Salma was his big sister and he was proud to have Zaman as his real father. Uzaid reassured Zaman that his mother had no other love interests. The children accepted and understood but conspired with their father to prolong his convalescence a while longer.

CHAPTER TWELVE

Naj is Home

It was Friday. A week had passed since the rainy night. Mai was still busy helping Asma. They were preparing for the baby's Akikah. The head had to be shaven, the two sheep had to be killed and there was to be cooking aand sharing of the meat and more cooking of sweetmeats. Shaheed had come to take Salma and Uzaid to help Grandma and Aunty Asma. It was 2.00pm. Bibi had cleaned up the house. She took a long bath and washed her hair and put on a light white cotton kaftan. She liked Friday. It was called the Eid of the week. Bibi left strong doses of tablets for the not so sick Zaman so that he would be asleep for hours and she could relax with a new novel she found at the supermarket. She was planning to enjoy a lazy Friday afternoon. She decided to look in on her patient first before putting her feet up on the sofa. He looked quite asleep. She walked past his bed and gently touched his hair. She smiled to herself thinking how successful she was to drug him off to an entire afternoon of sleep. She touched his nose lightly and said playfully, "Sweet dreams my Dear", and she turned to leave. Zaman was fully awake waiting for her. He had not taken any of her tablets. As she turned to go he grabbed her hand and pulled her to him. She was so surprised she fell with all her weight on top of him. She heard him say Ouch as he cradled her back and moved her gently to the side of him. He lay on his side looking at her. He played with her hair and ran his fingers over her eyes and nose and mouth. She felt warm all over and closed her eyes in modesty and shyness. He let his fingers trace each soft curve and then he leaned over and teased her some more. His lips were soft and his tongue probing and playful as he licked and tasted and licked and tasted her mouth. He felt her breathing quicken and her small body arch to meet him. Zaman could not deny his heart. He claimed her mouth with passion and hunger and held her to him as tightly as the stitches would allow. He then turned to look at her again. She opened her eyes and looked up at him. She was going to speak but he put a finger on her lips. "My beautiful Naj has come home," he said. It was not a question but a statement of how things were. She put her fingers through his beard and stroked it. She ran her fingers down his neck to his chest and played with the fields of curly hair. She kissed her way down to the long healing scar on his abdomen. He reached for her and kissed her, drinking in her sweetness, giving her his weakness and sharing in the hope. He watched her undress and stroke every part of his hungriness. Her touch was the balm he had been seeking all these years. They lay covered under a sheet. His Naj was home. The thought itself erected him and Naj could feel him pressing in need against her. She missed him. She missed the feel of him and the smell of him. He passionately took her mouth and all off her at the same time. As they lay close she pulled his head to lay on her bosom. "I love you so much," he heard her whisper in his ear. "I know", he said. He could feel her love in her touch, in her look. He kissed her closed eyes and told her gently, "Look at me Naj". She opened her eyes to him. "I love you Najma Abdool. You are my wife and the mother of my children," he said sweetly and quietly. He took her hand and placed it above his heart. She could feel the fast rhythmic beat. She knew his love was true.

They claimed each other in need and guilt and compensation and for whatever reason it had to be to overcome ten years of separation. Some time later Naj stood with her husband under the shower gently soaping and scrubbing all over. It was a divine feeling to stand naked crushed to him, feeling him own every part of her and seeing him satisfied and happy.

EPILOGUE

Grandma Mai came out of the labor room of the hospital and took the surgical mask off, announcing, "Zaman, you have two more mouths to feed." Naj had delivered twin boys. Zaman laughed as he held them. "More hands on the farm", he said. No one held any grudges and life continued with the Abdool family. Naj and Zaman were married again in a simple Nikah. Mai did not go back to New York but her son Zaheer was coming to visit with his wife and new baby girl.

Salma completed High School and she was training to become a Mathematics Teacher. Uzaid was in High School. Naj did charity work at clinics around the country. She did go back to the USA to settle with her job and apartment. Zaman had a US Permanent Resident status and Salma became a US citizen because her mother was. They traveled once a year to the USA but their lives developed in their tropical home.

Zaman and the children joined Naj in the hospital room. Naj looked at their happy faces. She was so thankful in her heart that all was well. She prayed with every sincere fibre of her being. Zaman was looking at her. He knew she was tired but he knew that look and he knew she was praying in her beautiful heart.

"Oh my Allah", Naj cried, "You are the Forgiver and the Most Merciful. You brought me back to my family and you brought my family back to me. Bless these two boys you have given us today that they would serve you and please you. Please watch over us all and guide us rightly away from evil. Thank you my Allah for the love you give me for Zaman and the love you give him for me and bless our Nikah. Allah o Akbar, Allah o Akbar. Oh Allah you are the Greatest." She looked up across the room into the eyes of her husband. Together they said, "Ameen".

The End.

GLOSSARY

1. Alhamdulilah.   Praise be to Allah
2. Allah.   Name of the Creator and One God in Islam
3. Allaho Akbar.   Allah is the Greatest
4. Ameen.   Said at end of prayers. May Allah accept it.
5. Asr   Third prayer of Muslims done in the afternoon
6. Assalamualaikum Shortened form of Islamic greeting meaning
                    May the Peace and Blessings of Almighty
                    Allah be with you.
7. Bismillah   In the name of Allah
8. Dastakan   Mat placed on the floor to put food on
9. Duaa   Prayer to Allah
10. Eid   First day of Shawaal, end of Ramadhan.
11. Esha   Fifth Muslim prayer done at night
12. Iftar   Meal to break the fast in Ramadhan
13. Inshallah   By the will of Allah
14. Magrib   Fourth Muslim prayer at sunset
15. Masjid   Muslim house of worship
16. Nikah   Muslim marriage ceremony
17. Qiyam   Opening action of salaat, both hands held to ears.
18. Quran   Holy Book of Muslims
19. Rakaats   Individual modules of prayer
20. Ramadhan   Ninth month of Muslim year for fasting
21. Salaat   Prayer of Muslims
22. Shawaal   Tenth month of Muslim year
23. Sunnah   According to the practice of Prophet
                    Muhammad(s.a.w)

24. Taraweeh	Twenty modules of prayer after Esha in Ramadhan
25. Waalaikumasalam	Shortened form of reply to greeting by Muslim
26. Zikr	Remembrance of Allah

www.ingramcontent.com/pod-product-compliance
Lightning Source LLC
Chambersburg PA
CBHW020255290526
45784CB00003B/1269